Six days of the Iris

L. G. Redmond-Howard

Alpha Editions

This edition published in 2023

ISBN : 9789357958943

Design and Setting By
Alpha Editions
www.alphaedis.com
Email - info@alphaedis.com

Contents

INTRODUCTION

The following pages are an attempt at a simple narrative and criticism of what must appear the most inexplicable occurrence in Irish history.

The climax of a century of arguments, futile only because of the proverbial dullness of the race to which they were addressed, the rising has lifted the Home Rule controversy at one stroke from the region of the village pump into the very midst of the counsels of Europe, for it was a challenge—of madmen, if you like—to the greatest Empire in the world, at the very moment of its gravest crisis, upon the most fundamental portion of its policy of interference with the affairs of the Continent, namely, England's claim to be the champion of small nationalities.

Unless Ireland can be shown to be held by her own free consent, in perfect contentment, the whole of our contention falls to the ground—for our policy in Ireland is only in microcosm our policy of Empire; and Germany will be able to point the finger of scorn and ridicule at us, and prove thereby to France and Russia that, tyrants at home, we only used them to fight a battle we dared not fight alone.

I say nothing here of the motives that inspired the rebels, nor the immediate causes that provoked them to rise, nor the nature of the methods by which they were "stamped out"; I only state the moral of their failure, and I must take this opportunity to thank Lord Decies, the official Press censor, for the freedom with which he has allowed me to speak at what I feel to be a very critical juncture in the history of my country and of our common Empire; for I have gone upon the principle that it is far better to distribute the blame all round than to try and make the Sinn Feiners the scapegoats of faults which each party contributed towards the catastrophe.

There never was, I believe, an Irish crime—if crime it can be called—which had not its roots in an English folly; and I repeat here what the late Mr. Stead always impressed upon me: Ireland is our school of Empire, and the mistakes which would lose us Ireland would lose us the Empire.

It is England's move next: we have protested in blood; the eyes of Europe await her decision.

At the same time I cannot help blaming Irishmen as well for the catastrophe, for politicians of all parties have been tending towards isolating their followers in the old ancestral bigotries, instead of drawing them together in sympathy, as Mr. William O'Brien has been advocating for years, with the result that we are now threatened with permanent constitutional separation for another generation.

It is a mistake which all the younger men deplore, and which could easily have been avoided by bringing in the men of Ulster into the national deliberations, as they have every right, in the name of their Southern followers, and then giving them the option to veto the application of any measure to their own districts—which would have been the best guarantee of justice which the Nationalists could have given and the most they had a right to expect of England, whose political position of dependence upon the Irish vote is a scandal of empire.

These things, however, are beyond the scope of the present pages, and I shall confine myself with thanking those of my many friends who have helped me in compiling this volume—notably Councillor Keogh, who was with me during the Battle of Mount Street Bridge, and others, whose criticisms helped me considerably. Likewise I must thank my publishers and Mr. O'Keefe, of O'Keefe's Press-cutting Agency; and Mr. George Atkinson, who designed the cover, and Mr. Crampton Walker; and also Mr. Marsh, the manager of the Coliseum, with whom I had several dangerous adventures while in Sackville Street; and lastly, those among my Sinn Fein friends who enabled me to get an inner view of a movement to which I have endeavoured to do the best of justice—that of a true statement of their intentions.

L. G. REDMOND-HOWARD.

T.C.D.,
   1916.

CHAPTER THE FIRST

A BOLT FROM THE BLUE

Those who were in Dublin on Easter Monday 1916 were privileged to witness a scene which for dramatic setting and for paradoxical conception is certainly the most extraordinary of any of the long line of rebellions in Irish history, for at a time when it seemed almost universally admitted that "Separatism" was from an economic, racial, and military point of view utterly impossible, there suddenly arose without warning, without apparent reason, and as if from nowhere, a body of men, fully armed and completely organized, who within the space of a single hour had captured every strategic point in the capital, and to its utter amazement held it up in the name of a new "Republic," in much the same way as a highwayman of old used to hold up coaches on Hounslow Heath.

It was in very deed a bolt from the blue. The first intimation that the general public got of the rising was the sudden spread of the wildest rumours—"Dublin Castle has just been taken by the Irish Volunteers," "The Post Office has been captured by the Sinn Feiners," "Soldiers and police are being shot at sight," "Larkin's Citizen Army are firing on women and children," but, for the most part, these rumours were discredited as impossible, at most being put down as some accidental clash between military and civilians, and it was only as people rushed into the street and heard the stories of the encounters first-hand that they began to realize that anything unusual was taking place.

Bodies of armed men had indeed been remarked in unusually large numbers in the streets all the morning, increasing and concentrating towards twelve, but everyone had grown so accustomed to these demonstrations for the past three years, since they had been inaugurated in Ulster by Sir Edward Carson, that nobody had taken any particular notice.

People merely remarked that it was rather strange, in view of the abandonment of the "Easter manœuvres" which had been organized for Sunday, and which had been cancelled at the last moment, late on Saturday night, by special order of Professor Eoin MacNeill, editor of the *Irish Volunteer*, which ran: "Owing to the very critical position, all orders given to Irish Volunteers for to-morrow, Easter Sunday, are hereby rescinded, and no parades, marches, or other movements of Irish Volunteers will take place. Each individual Volunteer will obey this order strictly in every particular."

It was supposed, therefore, that the numbers were due to the new recruits which had been the outcome of the protest against the deportation of the Sinn Fein leaders some time previous to this, and moderate people hoped that the Sinn Fein authorities were about to show the same discretion in the matter of an armed demonstration in Dublin which the authorities had shown in the matter of the proposed inclusion of the military in the St. Patrick's Day parade in Cork.

Possibly they may have had secret information—for they had their spies in every department—that the long-meditated disarmament had been determined upon, and immediately decided to anticipate the offensive by a strong defensive of their own choosing. At any rate, Monday found them fully prepared, each in his proper place.

Accordingly, on the exact stroke of midday the Volunteers in Sackville Street were suddenly seen to stop short opposite the Post Office. "I was outside the building at the time," said an eye-witness of that now historic event, Mr. E. A. Stoker, the well-known Grafton Street jeweller, "and noticed a mixed crowd of, I should say, roughly, about one hundred men and boys, all armed, and half the number carrying old portmanteaux and parcels of every description. It is said that Connolly was leading.

"He called, 'Halt! Left turn! Come on.' The crowd then ran into the Post Office. I also followed. Several men crossed the counter and held revolvers at the officials' heads.

"One youth, intensely pale and nervous, put a revolver at my breast and said, 'Clear out.'

"I replied, 'What's up?'

"He said, 'Hands up, or I'll blow your heart out.'

"Up went my hands, and he backed me out to the entrance, and within five minutes everyone else had been bundled out in the same unceremonious way, and they were in possession."

Once in possession of the Post Office—which from its position and character was admirably suited for a general headquarters—the next thing was to fortify the place, for there was no knowing what had happened to the other enterprises which had been timed to take place simultaneously, or when the authorities would send out an armed force for its recapture. Next, a number of shots—all blank—were discharged with the purpose of clearing the streets of sightseers and inquisitive idlers. These had the desired effect, after which floor after floor of the Post Office was systematically occupied, the officials being either placed under arrest or allowed to disperse, as each case suggested fit to the commander, and the air began to reverberate with the sounds of crashing glass and masonry as the lower windows were turned into fortified loopholes with the aid of furniture and bags.

Meanwhile a small group of policemen stood near the Nelson Monument helpless, but one must evidently have telegraphed for help, for within a few minutes a small detachment of mounted lancers came riding up.

People stood breathless in expectation.

The insurgents just allowed the first line to get abreast of the Pillar, and then they opened fire; and at once a couple of saddles were emptied and the rest at once turned and galloped for all they were worth up in the direction of the Rotunda.

One poor fellow was killed outright and a horse shot dead; after which a great cheer went up from the crowd in the G.P.O., who proceeded to take off the harness and carry it in triumph back to headquarters, one of the rebels in uniform taking the young lancer's sword.

Immediately after this a tramway car was blown up with dynamite at the corner of North Earl Street, making a sort of barricade against any possible approach from Amiens Street Station, where the Belfast trains were expected to arrive.

By this time I was on the scene of the crisis myself, having only heard the news on my way into Trinity, which had been quickly occupied by the O.T.C., who were thus able to practically cut the chief line of communication of the rebels and command a huge area of important streets which would otherwise have presented the utmost difficulties to the advance of regular troops.

Only the military were allowed in College, and, anxious to be on the spot at what everybody then expected would be no more than an hour or so's brisk encounter, I took a car to the "Metropole" in order to be present when the Post Office was taken—the hotel actually adjoining and overlooking the building.

My own experience must have been that of thousands of people in Dublin, but I quote it, as I will quote it again, because I can personally testify to it.

Everyone at the hotel was in a state of consternation, for hardly six yards away the windows of the Post Office were crashing to the ground in the street, and at everyone bags of refuse were being piled up, and the muzzles of rifles were commanding all the windows of the hotel guests.

Several soldiers were staying at the "Metropole," and as I saw the Sinn Feiners watching us, I suggested their changing the khaki into mufti, if only for the safety of the civilians—for on all sides soldiers were being shot at sight by snipers—a suggestion which found acceptance, for most of the officers were young subalterns on leave, and therefore unarmed.

For a long time we could not tell what was going to happen; every minute we expected the soldiers or the constabulary, and peered anxiously out, but it seemed as if they were never coming, and men in the hotel were anxiously consulting what to do and women packing up their jewels.

The one man who all the while kept as cool as a cucumber was Mr. Oliver, the manager of the "Metropole."

At last there came a martial tap, tap at the glass door of the hall entrance, from an officer arrayed in green and gold, wearing cocked hat and feathers and high top-boots, with a sword in one hand and a revolver in the other.

Behind him were two minor officials, each armed with a loaded rifle of modern pattern, with bayonets fixed.

I was at Mr. Oliver's side at the time, and we could see that only a pane divided us from a whole line of them ranged along the pavement. Resistance was useless, and Mr. Oliver gave orders to admit them.

"We intend to commandeer your food supply," said the man in the cocked hat, "and I must ask you to show me the way to your provisions."

For a second Mr. Oliver hesitated. "Suppose I refuse?" he said.

"In that case I will take them and you too," was the reply, and then, addressing the two men, he added, "Men, do your duty," and they ransacked the place, while I took down a list of the goods they took.

Eventually the officer signed a receipt for the goods taken in the name of the Irish Republic, and Mr. Oliver, much to my disappointment, pocketed the precious document.

They left, and after a few minutes came back with a ten-pound note. Again I presented myself, and ventured one or two questions.

The looting had already begun, and children were wandering through the streets with toys and food and sweets.

"Surely," I said to the officer, "you do not approve of all this indiscriminate theft?"

"No, certainly not," was his dignified reply.

I next asked the meaning of all the rising, and to this he simply replied:—

"It means that Ireland is free, that English government is at an end, and that we have established an Irish Republic. As it is, we hold the whole city, and within a few days the provinces will be ours as well."

I still pressed for a pronouncement on the real aims and objects of the new Government, and was referred to headquarters.

Accordingly, I took my courage in both hands and walked past the soldiers opposite the Post Office and the sandbagged windows, and asked the guard at the main door if I could have an interview with their President.

At first I thought I was going to get it, but I suddenly noticed a change come over the man, and saw guns covering me in a most uncomfortable way.

I argued my case with some of the minor officials, and pleaded the importance of such a pronouncement, but, taking me possibly for a spy, I was ordered off, and told that my safest way was to get back to my hotel, where no harm would come to me as a civilian if only I left the men of action alone.

As soon as I realized the impossibility of penetrating the headquarters, I returned to the "Metropole" and took up a position of vantage upon the balcony, and was able to secure a unique snapshot of the hoisting of the new flag of the Republic, and took another of the cheering of the crowd—though this was very insignificant and in no way represented any considerable body of citizens, any of the better class having disappeared, leaving the streets to idlers and women and children or else stray sightseers.

This was certainly a thing that struck me, and I realized at once that the movement was at that time a dismal failure as far as the vast majority of Nationalist Ireland was concerned. There was practically no response whatever from the people: it seemed the very antithesis of the emancipation of a race as we see it, say, in the capture of the Bastille in the French Revolution. They looked on partly with amazement, partly with curiosity—waiting for something dramatic to happen.

The point struck me with particular pathos—there they were posing as the saviours of their country, and yet there they were already doomed before they had even struck a single blow—and doomed by the verdict of their own countrymen.

As I was making the remark to one of the men in the hotel, a boy with a handful of sheets issued from the Post Office—they were the proclamation of the new Republic of Ireland.

Instead of eagerly scanning the sheets and picking out the watchwords of the new liberty, or glowing with enthusiastic admiration at the phrases or sentiments, most of the crowd "bought a couple as a souvenir"—some with the cute business instinct "that they'd be worth a fiver each some day, when the beggars were hanged."

I give another pathetic story told to me, though I cannot vouch for it. It was that young Plunkett was deputed to go to the base of Nelson's Pillar and there read out the new charter of liberty to the emancipated citizens.

He read it with deep emotion to a pack of squabbling women and children—and he had hardly half finished the document when suddenly there was a crash, followed by the sound of breaking glass.

At once the crowd turned round and looked in the direction whence it proceeded, and one old woman, half sodden with drink, exclaimed with delight, "Hooroosh!—they're raiding Noblet's toffee-shop." Whereupon the newly emancipated slaves of a foreign tyranny rushed to partake in the orgy of sweetmeats which came tumbling out into the street.

It was to me the saddest picture of the whole revolution, and even if not true, was certainly typical of much of the pathos which crowned this mixture of humour and tragedy.

The document in question, however, was by no means undignified, taken as an explanation of the ideals that animated the rebels, but it was simply ridiculous when judged by the hard common-sense standards of stern reality, though it was probably never meant for anything more than a rhetorical protest in the name of the fast-ebbing sense of Nationality.

This Utopian outburst perhaps speaks best for itself, and I quote it in full:—

POBLACHT NA H-EIREANN.
THE PROVISIONAL GOVERNMENT
OF THE
IRISH REPUBLIC
TO THE PEOPLE OF IRELAND.

Irishmen and Irishwomen: In the name of God and of the dead generations from which she receives her old traditions of nationhood, Ireland, through us, summons her children to her flag and strikes for her freedom. Having organized and trained her manhood through her secret revolutionary organization, the Irish Republican Brotherhood, and through her open military organizations, the Irish Volunteers and the Irish Citizen Army; having patiently perfected her discipline, having resolutely waited for the right moment to reveal itself, she now seizes that moment, and, supported by her exiled children in America and by gallant Allies in Europe, but relying in the first place on her own strength, she strikes in full confidence of victory.

We declare the right of the people of Ireland to the ownership of Ireland, and to the unfettered control of Irish destinies, to be sovereign and indefeasible. The long usurpation of that right by a foreign people and Government has not extinguished the right, nor can it ever be extinguished except by the destruction of the Irish people. In every generation the Irish people have asserted their right to national freedom and sovereignty; six times during the past three hundred years they have asserted it in arms. Standing on that fundamental right and again asserting it in arms in the face of the world, we hereby proclaim the Irish Republic as a sovereign independent State, and we pledge our lives and the lives of our comrades in arms to the cause of its freedom, of its welfare, and of its exaltation among the nations.

The Irish Republic is entitled to and hereby claims the allegiance of every Irishman and Irishwoman. The Republic guarantees religious and civil liberty, equal rights, and equal opportunities to all its citizens, and declares its resolve to pursue the happiness and prosperity of the whole nation and of all its parts, cherishing all the children of the nation equally and oblivious of the differences carefully fostered by an alien Government, which have divided a minority from the majority in the past.

Until our arms have brought the opportune moment for the establishment of a permanent national Government representative of the whole people of Ireland and elected by the suffrages of all her men and women, the Provisional Government hereby constituted will administer the civil and military affairs of the Republic in trust for the people.

We place the cause of the Irish Republic under the protection of the Most High God, whose blessing we invoke upon our arms, and we pray that none who serves that cause will dishonour it by cowardice, inhumanity, or rapine. In this supreme hour the Irish nation must, by its valour and discipline, and by the readiness of its children to sacrifice themselves for the common good, prove itself worthy of the august destiny to which it is called.

Signed on behalf of the Provisional Government:—

THOMAS J. CLARKE.

SEAN MacDIARMADA.

THOMAS MacDONAGH.

J. H. PEARSE.   EAMONN CEANNT.

JAMES CONNOLLY.   JOSEPH PLUNKETT.

But to continue the narrative. According to a young woman cleric in the G.P.O. the Sinn Feiners had chosen the place for their headquarters partly because they were already familiar with the place, which was proved by the way they settled down each to his own work the moment they entered it, and partly because they had already made it a storehouse.

All this while much the same process was going on all over the city. The attack upon the Castle was hardly less dramatic than that upon the G.P.O., but it seems to have been undertaken by fewer troops of Volunteers and carried out less cleverly, so that it eventually fell back into the hands of the military. I believe it was originally intended to burn the place to the ground, as symbolical of the centuries of tyranny with which it has been associated. Strategically it might not have been of such value to the insurgents, but the moral effect of its capture would undoubtedly have been enormous upon the provinces if they had been able to telegraph it within the first few hours of the rising.

The Castle, however, had never formed the main point of attack; it was at most an emotional side-issue. The scheme for the defence of Dublin was a far greater conception, and there was hardly a bookseller in the city, as I learnt later from Fred Hanna, of Nassau Street, whose shop had not been visited during the past few weeks by one or other of the insurgent leaders with the object of securing all the standard works on strategy and military operations—which rather goes to prove that the step had been long in contemplation.

The idea seems to have been to draw a cordon around the city by securing first of all the chief railway stations and the larger dominating buildings, such as Jacob's biscuit factory, and then to man the corner houses that overlooked the main roadways at the point where they crossed the canals, and thus prevent all approach of the military till messengers should be dispatched from Dublin to tell the counties to rise.

Probably the greatest disappointment to the rebels was the capture of the famous Magazine Fort in the Phœnix Park.

It was generally understood that this was crammed to the very door with guns and ammunition—heavy guns especially—and the most elaborate preparations had consequently been made for its capture, the idea probably being that once Ireland had heard of the capture of Dublin there would be a general movement from the country towards the capital, and that the new recruits could be fitted out from the magazine and then dispatched to provincial headquarters. It was probably for this reason the long line of the quays along the Liffey had been kept clear—the Four Courts being a sort of halfway fort.

The loss of the Magazine Fort—or rather the failure of their expectation in its regard, for it was found to be practically empty when searched—meant that they were bound to depend entirely upon Germany for the larger ammunition. The railways were of course of supreme importance, and simultaneously with the raid of the Post Office, Jacob's, and the Castle, attacks were made on all the principal stations.

At twelve prompt Westland Row was occupied without a struggle and the doors closed, sentinels being placed on the bridge spanning the street below—arousing no little local curiosity, for the news had not circulated through the town by this time.

Harcourt Street Station was also taken over and an attempt made to fortify it, but this was abandoned after some time, quite early in the afternoon. Broadstone Station also fell before the insurgents; but neither the attempt upon Amiens Street or Kingsbridge, where the soldiers from Belfast and the Curragh would necessarily arrive, succeeded. The military did not secure the former without a struggle, having to stand a siege, while the latter's approaches were kept clear by means of an engine, on which several armed snipers were placed, and which was kept moving continually up and down, sweeping the country of any Sinn Feiners who might attempt to approach in order to tamper with the permanent way.

This was rendered necessary because immediately the rebels got possession of a line their first steps were to destroy signalling points and junctions, and in one or two instances, such as on the Kingstown line, actually tore up the permanent way, while in several other places attempts were made to blow up the bridges with dynamite.

Had it not been for this the whole coup might have been ended on Monday or Tuesday at latest, instead of dragging on day after day.

Every bridge across the canal which bounds Dublin on the south was commanded by corner-houses, entered at the point of the revolver and turned, in spite of all protest, into fortresses in an almost mediæval fashion.

Liberty Hall, from whence floated the green emblem which had first been hoisted when the four Labour leaders were deported, was a sort of central storehouse of munitions, and was strongly guarded, but strange to say the Custom House on the other side of the railway was left untouched.

This was probably because the docks were sufficiently defended by the factories, like Ringsend and Boland's bakery, vast straggling buildings on either side of the railway approach, and which were not only occupied, but stored with food and ammunition and loopholed and sandbagged to stand a fortnight's siege if necessary.

The one great mistake made by the rebels appears to have been the occupation of Stephen's Green, a huge open square, which, surrounded as it is by tall buildings on all four sides, was bound to become a death-trap, and eventually did so become.

At exactly the same time as the Post Office was occupied, Volunteers entered the famous square, which might almost be called a park, and ordered the civilians out at the point of the revolver. They then proceeded to entrench themselves and make barricades of any convenient object, seizing trams, cabs, benches, and even holding up motor-cars and turning them to this purpose.

In the carrying out of this several civilians were shot at and wounded, either by accidental shots meant for soldiers or for refusing obedience to the new self-constituted authorities.

Great carts, filled presumably with ammunition, were next escorted into the Green, and then the doors were locked and barred and tied very strongly, and finally the ropes greased—which shows how carefully almost any eventuality had been planned.

Whether their danger on the Green dawned upon them in time I cannot say, but when they saw themselves dominated by the great roof of the Shelbourne Hotel—about half an hour after the seizure of the open square for a camp—a rush was made for the hotel, which luckily had just been captured in the nick of time by a few of the military, who immediately began to fire on the rebels below, at the same time guarding the doors. A short while afterwards the main body of new Sinn Fein arrivals were noticed to make their way, instead, to the Royal College of Surgeons at the opposite end, which became one of their most stoutly defended strongholds under the famous Countess Markievicz.

Two further mistakes of the most vital importance were made in the rebels' plan for the capture of Dublin, however, which were eventually to be the deciding factor of the whole situation, and to which more than anything they must be said to owe the sudden collapse of their movement as well in the capital as in the provinces. The first was the omission to capture the telephone system after securing the telegraphs so completely.

This meant not only that the military authorities could still keep in touch with the few troops that still remained in Ireland, but it meant that the authorities at the Castle were able to get into touch with London.

One can hardly imagine the chaos that would have ensued if, for example, a delay of a couple of days had had to intervene between the occurrence of the rising and communication with London—which might have been quite possible, since they held the wireless stations as well as the cables, and German submarines were supposed to be watching the mail boats.

The other great mistake was to allow Trinity College, which was the strategic key to Dublin City, to fall into the hands of a few of the Officers' Training Corps, who must be given the credit of saving the capital from total capture and Grafton Street from pillage.

For as long as this was held by soldiers all the internal lines of communication of the rebels were blocked and they themselves threatened on all sides.

Otherwise the republicans had complete control of the city: the police were confined to barracks, civilians were on all sides at the mercy of a perfectly organized and armed body of revolutionaries all in touch with a headquarter staff, and the military, somewhere beyond the outskirts of the city, were—nobody knew exactly where, and the whole population on all sides hushed in expectation of the inevitable battle.

For it had ceased to be a mere riot: it had become a revolution.

CHAPTER THE SECOND

JUST BEFORE THE BATTLE

Those who went through that period of anxious expectancy between Monday afternoon and Wednesday morning, knowing themselves absolutely at the mercy of what appeared to be a "secret society suddenly gone mad and in possession of the reins of government," will never forget the experience.

The whole thing was so sudden, so unprecedented, so inexplicable that the intelligence simply refused to perform the ordinary functions of thought.

Everywhere civilians were being bullied into obedience at the point of the bayonet: young boys in their teens brandished revolvers in the high roads: rough, brawny dockers walked about endowed apparently with unlimited authority, and in the dark recesses of the General Post Office, beyond the reach of law or argument, the mysterious Republican Brotherhood—omnipotent.

All the while stories were coming in of hairbreadth escapes, of stray shots, apparently from the sky, picking off unfortunate wayfarers, and of whole parties of officers on their way back from the races in their cars being captured and held up by the Volunteers—and every story went one further than the one before it, till one was ready to believe almost anything.

Personally, I kept within the "Metropole," expecting every minute that the "climax" of the situation would be reached, but still the soldiery did not arrive, and we began to come to the belief that in all probability the authorities were only waiting until dusk.

I could not tear myself from the windows. That instinct of expectation gripped me like a vice, and continued to do so for twenty-four solid hours—and if I quote my own experience it is only as an example of what others all around me went through.

It was now about four o'clock, and still I looked out into the street below—the people were beginning to go wild with excitement, for every now and then the Sinn Feiners would fire blank cartridges, and each time they did so, with the one cry "The soldiers are coming!" a mass of several thousand men, women, and children would rush now to one end of Sackville Street, now to the other. After Noblet's it was the Saxon Shoe Company and Dunn's hat-shop's turn to be looted, and one could see little guttersnipe wearing high silk hats and new bowlers and straws, who had never worn headgear before: bare-footed little devils with legs buried in Wellington top-boots, unable to bend their knees, and drunken women brandishing satin shoes and Russian boots till it seemed as if the whole revolution would collapse in ridicule or pandemonium. For there was no animosity in the crowd at first, just as there was no enthusiasm—certainly no avarice or desire for theft—only sheer demoralization and mischief for mischief's sake: but every hour it became worse. Sometimes there was absolutely no point in the loot. I saw an urchin of nine brandishing with pride More's "Utopia" and Wells's "New Machiavelli," which he compared with a rival urchin's—a girl's—bunch of newspapers on "Poultry" and "Wireless," and solemnly exchanging their treasures.

I saw a tussle between two drunken harlots for the possession of a headless dummy taken from a draper's shop, and noted a youngster go up to the very steps of the Provisional Government House of the New Republic of Ireland and amuse the armed rebels with impersonations of Charlie Chaplin.

In another portion of the street I saw a drunken sailor mad with hate make a furious assault upon a woman, and then, when the crowd yelled in horror, suddenly change his mind from murder and kiss his victim: while in yet another portion of the street a woman of about sixty was kneeling with hands outstretched to heaven, clasping a rosary and crying her prayers to the Mother of God in heaven for "Ireland to be a nation once again!"

Time after time I felt inclined to weep with very shame at the whole thing; for as I passed a group of young English *revue* girls who had come along to see the "show," I heard one exclaim, "A little bit of heaven, and they call it Ireland!" and everyone laughed; and another threw out the gibe: "Irish, and proud of it, eh?"

They were not meant as insults—no, certainly not—merely the happy laughing cynicism of the common-sense view that would be taken of us by hundreds of cartoonists; but I must say they went through me as hardly anything else I witnessed, for they showed in such a terrible light the contrast between the dream that had inspired these men and the reality that they had brought forth.

Meantime, however, things were maturing, and as they matured the ridiculous element faded and the tragic element began to come into the picture.

Every few minutes dispatch riders would come up on motor-cycles to the Post Office, and emerge a few minutes later with sealed orders. A long line of motor-cars "held up" at the point of the revolver was also requisitioned and placed at the disposal of the rebels in a queue before the Post Office side-entrance. Then came the supplies of food and ammunition on huge lorries from the country districts, each with its escort of six young farmers fully armed, with double bandoliers filled to bursting-point with cartridges; and as I stood outside the *Freeman* offices, just at the side-gate of the "fortress," I was amazed at the regularity of the whole proceeding: password, cheques, guards, orders, everything, in fact, went off without the slightest hitch. And no wonder—as I found out later—for during the past few weeks nearly every manœuvre had been rehearsed in mufti by the Volunteers, acting under the orders of their chiefs, and each man knew his position, his work, and the exact minute at which he was to perform it.

In this way, at a given signal it had been possible to hold up the whole city of Dublin with the ease of a highwayman holding up a coach on a lonely common in Georgian days.

I shall never forget the awful growing stillness of that afternoon as the hours flew by, for all traffic was at an end. Now and again in the general silence one heard the crack of a rifle, the hoot of a captured motor and the cry "Stop, in the name of the Irish Republic!" from the Volunteers, and the ghastly howling of the mob as more shop-fronts gave way—but all these sounds came spasmodically and only intensified the surrounding stillness. And all the while everyone was expecting the arrival of the military, and saying, "When will the soldiers come?" Then, "Will the soldiers come?" and later, "Will the soldiers never come?"

Soon dusk began to come on more rapidly, and we conjectured that the authorities must have determined to wait till dark. The Volunteers, too, felt this, and took up positions on the roof and strengthened their outposts, every hour or so a dozen or two Volunteers fully armed going off from the Post Office.

The "Metropole" being situated alongside the Post Office, I could not get any direct view of what I knew would be the centre of the battle, and so I determined to move across to the "Imperial," which, situated *vis-à-vis* the Post Office on the top of Clery's Stores, commanded the fullest view of the rebel headquarters.

There I found everyone, including the manager, Mr. Woods, in the same state of bewilderment as at the "Metropole."

I mentioned who I was, and was told that a priest in the smoking-room had just heard that John Redmond had been captured by the Sinn Feiners and had, in all probability, been shot—but this was only one of the thousand rumours that were by this time flying about the city, another being that the Castle was in flames, with the Lord-Lieutenant in the middle of the inner yard, and yet another describing the heroic death of Father O'Doherty of Marlborough Street, who was supposed to have been shot through the head in full vestments, having endeavoured to remonstrate, cross in hand, with the rebels, in order to persuade them to lay down their arms in the name of God.

The street was now (9.30) in a perfect state of pandemonium, for a fire had begun in the premises of the Cable Shoe Company, which immediately adjoined Clery's, and hence was an imminent danger to us.

I rushed down, and to my amazement found that the place, already looted, had been set on fire deliberately, and that there was not one of the crowd of two hundred spectators who seemed to be aware of, or even to care about, the fate of the flat over the shop, which from the look of the curtains appeared to be inhabited.

The cellars were crackling as if they contained some fatty, resinous substance, purposely placed there with incendiary intent, and the smoke was blinding and suffocating. The door of the side entrance was locked and I could not force it, so I called for a few volunteers to try to break it down by ramming it with some planks that were lying about, and though we did not succeed in breaking it, we were able to arouse the attention of the sleepers, and a dentist popped his head out and told us there were women and children in the house.

Some by this time had run off for the fire-engine, and others, realizing the danger, helped us to carry the inmates to safety, one woman being actually in her confinement and frightened almost to death. After that we rescued a few personal belongings with difficulty, but the smoke was too terrible to do more, and the stairs were perfectly hot; and so I went back with the owner to the hotel, where the family were put up and given clothes, having been forced to rise from their beds.

Soon after this I met Mr. Marsh, the manager of the Coliseum, who told me that the rebels had just commandeered the building, which immediately backs the Post Office, and had placed a guard at the door to prevent looting.

As a matter of fact, as we afterwards found out, it was merely to secure the building as a means of retreat in case of a rout of their headquarters at the Post Office—with the result that the building is now burnt to the ground by naval shells, which pursued the rebels in their retreat.

Sleep on such a night was of course out of the question—we did not know at what time the military would arrive—but in any case we secured a room on the second floor, looking into the street, for we were determined to see the thing out, still never dreaming but that the whole thing would be over within a few dramatic hours. Meanwhile the street below became worse and worse. On all sides now the looters came up from the black depths of the slums like packs of hungry wolves, so that every minute we expected that Clery's underneath would be the next to go. Indeed, over at Mansfield's opposite we heard one of the crowd telling the looters to go over and smash William Martin Murphy's windows—Murphy was one of the directors of Clery's—and reminding them that it was he, Boss Murphy, was the real enemy of the people—"the man who caused the lock-out in the days of Jim Larkin"; but the looters, having tasted the blood of theft, were far too avaricious by this time to think of politics in their orgy, and instead began to make a raid on a tobacco-shop, and next a small jeweller's. One could see small boys, too, going to the outskirts of the crowd to sell the booty, so that those who had not the pluck to steal salved their consciences by buying the loot, in most cases getting some fifteen or twenty shillings' worth for as many farthings.

About twelve the Sinn Feiners, without directly encouraging loot, unconsciously helped it by the order to "barricade the side streets," and for hours nothing could be heard but the crash of furniture being pitched into the street below from second, third, and fourth story windows, till the barricades were eight or ten feet high, composed of chairs, tables, desks, sofas, beds, and all kinds of furniture and stores.

In one place, "Kelly's" of Abbey Street, hundreds of cycles and motor cycles were piled up—at least five thousand pounds' worth—and brand-new motor-cars were then run into it, thus forming a steel wall of solid machinery, upon which, later in the "war," the rebels poured petrol and set the whole pile alight, with the result that the neighbouring houses, hotels, and eventually the Hibernian Academy, with its five hundred pictures, were burnt to the ground.

As the early hours of the morning approached the crowd began to disperse, the most enthusiastic singing the latest music-hall songs, and soon O'Connell Street became black and deserted, save for a few specks of candlelight moving about in the G.P.O., which was otherwise in complete darkness, and a few guards marching up and down beneath the great Greek portico.

We retired then to our own room to watch and think. Never to my dying day shall I ever forget those long hours of midnight stillness, broken only by the distant rattle of the rifles in the direction of Phœnix Park, where the two forces had by this time come into contact.

One could easily distinguish the crack of the respective rifles: the Government weapons had a harsher and lower note, but for each "spit" of the rebel guns one could hear the dread rattle of the military machine guns;

and then we knew that there could only be one possible end—defeat, ignominious and complete.

Before us, hardly fifty yards away, stood the Post Office, lit up by the street arc lamps in pale blues and greens, and looking for all the world like the drop-cloth of a theatre; and there were we, it might have been the dress circle of some gigantic opera house, and the feeling—the feeling was excruciatingly morbid. We felt like cynical critics sent to review a drama foredoomed to fiasco, yet with the difference that the actors were all real and that the tragedy would be enacted in the blood of hundreds of innocent lives.

We were watching the climax of years of planning and the culminating point of so many lifetimes of idealism, effort, and sacrifice, however mistaken.

We knew they would fail: we knew the penalty of the failure—the traitor's death or the convict's cell; but we were held to the spot, to see just how "dramatic" the fiasco would be.

The very thought was a continuous torture, and it haunted us like a ghost or a madness.

We knew they were our own flesh and blood that had rebelled: it would be strangers who would conquer, and yet we knew that order was right: and this too was a torture-thought.

Hour after hour passed, and when I was not at the window Marsh was on watch, and when he was asleep I mounted my pensive guard.

Incidents never ceased, but the incidents were as nothing compared with the reflections they aroused.

Hour after hour unarmed Volunteers came in from the country, stayed in an hour or so, and then moved out armed. Carts and cars of ammunition and food arrived and gave the password and were admitted. As the early hours of dawn approached we could see milk and bread carts driving up at top speed, the driver with the cold muzzle of a revolver at his ear and his captors seated behind him.

Sometimes flash signals would shoot across the sky, and at others a man at the "Metropole" corner of the G.P.O. would open a basket and release carrier pigeons, so complete was their organization.

At daybreak we found our room covered by a guard, with rifles pointed at our heads, the light shining over their backs full into our faces: but we made no movement, and an hour or so later moved to another portion of the roof.

Next the street was cleared and barbed wire stretched across.

About six o'clock we saw Connolly emerge at the head of a band, and we could hear one of his subordinates call out Mr. Connolly this and Mr. Connolly that, and the commander-in-chief give his orders in a clear, resonant, and fearless voice.

About eight we thought our last hour had come, for, looking towards the base of Nelson's Pillar, we saw men running from a thin blue spiral of smoke rising up, followed by a terrific explosion. They were trying to blow up the monument.

So Tuesday had come, but it found the situation no further advanced: the military had not come: the rebels had had time to entrench and fortify themselves: the city was really fully in their possession: but the battle had begun.

We could now hear it in the direction of the Castle and the Four Courts, and we thought it could only be a matter of a few hours before they would reach Sackville Street, for we could hear the military machine guns raking Dame Street from Trinity College.

As a matter of fact, a machine gun had been hoisted upon the roof of the Hibernian Bank, which commanded the old Houses of Parliament, upon which the rebels had climbed, and in the space of a few seconds wiped out the whole contingent.

As the afternoon wore on Sackville Street began to assume two totally distinct characteristics—one of tragedy and the other of comedy. South of the Pillar the scene might have been a battlefield; north of the Pillar it might have been a nursery gone tipsy, for by this time all the children of the slums had discovered that a perfect paradise of toys lay at their absolute mercy at Lawrence's bazaar, and accordingly a pinafore and knickerbocker army began to lay siege to it, the mothers taking seats upon the stiffened corpses of the lancers' horses to watch the sight of thousands of Union-jacks made into bonfires.

The scene was indescribable for chaos: there were men locked in deadly combat for the sake of Empire and Fatherland, and here were the very children they were fighting for—some dying for—revelling in a children's paradise of toys—balloons, soldiers, rackets, and lollypops, as if it had all been arranged for their special benefit.

An air-gun battalion was now formed of the young highwaymen—two guns each, one on each shoulder—followed up by a toy anti-aircraft gun on wheels, and the whole cavalcade brought up by a Noah's Ark the size of a perambulator.

The captain, about eight years of age, wore a blue silk waistcoat (with its price ticket) and a new grey silk hat. The band then formed up in Indian file, marched up to the G.P.O., saluted majestically, and then impertinently fired their pellets slap-bang into the faces of the insurgents, and then broke up and ran for all they were worth.

All the while, in the opposite direction, Red War was at its height: the rifle-fire along the quays was terrific, and ambulances were rushing backwards and forwards and relays of Volunteers were issuing from the central depôt to the firing-line.

Probably never in the world's history had there been such a strange combination of pathos and humour, and it will haunt everyone who saw it to their dying day: and if mere passive spectators felt the clash of divergent emotions how much more must these, for all their idealism must have appeared to them as crashing down at the first touch of reality.

It was so much the repetition of Emmet's revolt, ending in riot and loot and degradation—nay, worse, it seemed a very pantomime.

Suddenly, as the sound of maxims grew louder, a terrific black cloud rose into the sky. A fire had broken out in the heart of the bazaar and the flames had just reached the fireworks, and for a solid half-hour the whole gaze of rebel and civilian alike was centred upon Lawrence's, which presented the appearance of a diminutive Crystal Palace, with Catherine wheels, Roman candles, Chinese crackers going forth in all directions. At last, in a big blue, green, red and yellow bouquet, the main stock went bodily into the air, scattering the crowd of men and women head-over-heels over the dead horses, and all was still.

What the scene must have been like to the leaders, I do not dare to imagine: but it was so symbolical of the whole eruption that I cannot forbear to describe it.

It was shortly after this—about 4.30—that Mr. Marsh and myself came off the roof, where we had been four solid hours watching, tired, sad, and sick at heart. I was a mass of tingling nerves, for the whole thing was set in the background and framework of the penal days and the times of the famine. He was as cool as an icicle—he even suggested chess, and had a pocket set—but, chess in revolution?—what next!

We were not at a loss for our next course, however, for we had no sooner sat down to lunch—three hours late—than we noticed two of the Sinn

Feiners who had long watched us on the roof suddenly come across the street.

For one moment we made sure we were going to be taken out and shot for spies: for we had kept our eyes fixed on them twelve hours, and of course, as the telephone system still worked, could have kept in continual communication with the military authorities—it was the Sinn Feiners' one oversight, to leave the telephone intact—but we were soon reassured, for Mr. Woods came up and announced that the hotel had been taken over by the rebels.

The next moment the dining-room was invaded by a crowd who might have stepped direct off the French Revolution scenes of the "Scarlet Pimpernel" or "The Only Way," but their officer was perfectly courteous.

"Finish your meal, gentlemen," he said; "there is no hurry, but I must ask you to leave with all possible speed." And then, addressing his men, he added: "Now, then, two men to every window; take furniture, tables, chairs, anything, and barricade away—we may have to stand siege."

"Is there any immediate danger?" I ventured; "and if so, where do you wish us to go?"

"No immediate danger whatever, sir, save from your own resistance," was his reply. "Civilians are all perfectly safe: we are only fighting the troops of England.

"There is no cause for excitement or flurry," he added; "you may find our men firing over your heads as you pass into the street, but take no notice.

"These are partly our own signallers giving us warning, and also they are intended to clear the streets of loiterers. You will have safe conduct out of the city by the north, where our guards have orders to allow all citizens to pass—I can only counsel you to move as far from the city as possible, as it is more than probable that our positions will be shelled from the sea at any time, and gas bombs may be used in order to save the buildings, which I need not say would be equally fatal to civilians as to ourselves."

With that he asked the way to the fire-escape and the roof, which one of us showed him, and then we hastily made parcels of anything we wished to take with us.

I took occasion to get into conversation with one of the guards, a rough-looking fellow, upon the aims of the revolution, but could elicit nothing very intelligent, save that "England always hated Ireland, and that now was the time to free her, or within a couple of years everyone would be slaves and conscripts."

There seemed to be a rumour, too, that John Redmond had consented to conscription for Ireland and that it was to be passed at the secret session—but I could gather nothing definite, and before I could get further details a superior officer came and severely reprimanded him for allowing himself to be drawn into conversation at all.

There was nothing for it, therefore, but to march out, and as I could not cross a bridge to get back to the south side of the city, I accepted an offer of hospitality for the night with Mr. Marsh—provided I was willing to walk to Howth for it, nine miles away.

The rain was drizzling as we made our way into Sackville Street. Lawrence's was a blazing furnace, and on the roof we could see a woman and child, caught by the fire, trying to reach the ladders of the fire brigade, which were short; the side wall was tottering, there were screams, but I turned my head: I felt too sick to look, save at the gaping crowd, that even disgusted the rebels, who fired several blank shots among them in the vain attempt to scatter them.

As soon as we reached the Parnell Monument, close to the Rotunda, we turned to the right, and made our way through the long lines of tenements—refugees.

There was quite a string of refugees, as one might have seen fleeing from Ypres, for we knew that the place was now doomed to be shelled—it only remained the chance of a tossed coin where the blows would fall.

The rain poured down, but the seven of us, including the manager of the Coliseum and the manager of the "Imperial," who made up our party, trudged on, on, on. Every cross-road had its Sinn Fein sentries, every point of vantage was loopholed for miles around, and it was a mere stroke of luck that Annesley Bridge had not been blown up and so cut off Amiens Street Station, which held 300 troops, from the north. We only saw two soldiers in nine miles, and these were at a pier-head at Dollymount, half way.

When we arrived at Howth we were wet as fish and black as miners, for we finished the last couple of miles upon a charitable coal-cart.

The next morning was bright and warm as a midsummer day, but in the distance across the bay we could hear the sound of the naval guns thundering out shot and shell.

They had given the rebels till eight to surrender—and they had refused. It was no longer a riot—it was civil war.

CHAPTER THE THIRD

BATTLE

Monday and Tuesday were for the most part employed in clearing the streets and preparing the field for the battle which was to last continuously until late on Saturday evening, but it seems a pity, looking back on the situation, that the time was not employed in trying to avoid such a fatal issue; and that it would have been possible is proved by the example of Cork, where all conflict was avoided by a timely negotiation between the rebels and the ordinary civil and ecclesiastical authorities.

However, of this more later; it was decided to treat the matter in the sternest possible manner, which was just, as it turned out, what the Sinn Feiners wanted, and the military authorities, as it were, fell into the trap prepared for them by those astute politicians: for that they foresaw the political effects of ruthless suppression is now an admitted fact.

On Tuesday, April 25th, therefore, the day following the *coup*, the citizens of Dublin—or such as were not totally isolated—read in their morning *Irish Times* (the *Express* and the *Freeman* having ceased publication) two proclamations announcing the official English view of the rising, and people noted particularly the words that traced the attempt to subvert the supremacy of the Crown "to the foreign enemies of their King and country"—in a word, it was to be put down purely and simply to Germany.

As regards details, however, the inhabitants had to content themselves with the simple statement that "yesterday morning an insurrectionary rising took place in the City of Dublin"; that "the authorities had taken active and energetic measures to cope with the situation, which measures were proceeding favourably"; but this official condolence in their plight was rather discomforting, as the whole city was still in the possession of the insurgents.

Next, another proclamation was issued declaring the county of Dublin under martial law, warning all peaceable and law-abiding subjects within the area of the danger of frequenting or being in any place in the vicinity of which His Majesty's forces were engaged in the suppression of disorder, and enjoining upon them the duty and necessity of remaining so far as practicable within their own homes so long as such dangerous conditions prevailed, and proclaiming that all persons found carrying arms without lawful authority were liable to be dealt with severely by virtue of such proclamation.

All this, of course, was anything but reassuring, especially in view of the danger everybody felt of a provincial rising and the whispers of a German invasion; but towards the evening another statement was issued to the effect that the trouble was confined to Dublin and one or two other districts only in a minor way.

Yet the trouble was by no means even at its height.

All Tuesday the Sinn Feiners had been preparing for the inevitable battle, but these preparations merely took the shape of consolidating the positions already occupied.

At O'Connell Bridge, for example, Kelly's shop at the corner of Bachelors' Walk was garrisoned, and Hopkins's jewellery establishment at the opposite corner was similarly occupied.

In Lower Abbey Street, opposite Wynn's Hotel, a formidable barricade was erected, composed partly of paper taken from the *Irish Times* store.

The wireless station was also seized, and all day long messages were flashed to the four corners of the world announcing the establishment of an Irish Republic, which messages were picked up at sea by special envoys who had been forewarned, and sent on till they finally reached New York and Petrograd.

The amazement of Russia and America must have been considerable— especially Russia's.

Yet it was not all preparation, for already the troops, or such as could be brought up in time, had come into contact with the Sinn Feiners on the outskirts of the town; but the chief activity appears to have been the strengthening of the position in Trinity College, which allowed the troops to form a wedge between Westland Row at one end and Dame Street on the other, thus cutting off Stephen's Green from Sackville Street.

On Monday night the danger in this quarter had been from the eastern side, but on Tuesday morning it was the College Green entrances that appeared most open to attack, and which were accordingly strengthened by sandbags within the windows of the main entrance and wings.

Irish Volunteer scouts on bicycles tried several times to get past through Grafton Street, but they could not get past the Colonial sharpshooters posted in the College, and tried by way of side streets, which were more or less covered by their own snipers, but in vain also.

Machine guns swept right up Dame Street on the one hand and on the other through Westmorland Street as far up as O'Connell's Statue at the end of the bridge; but this was as far north as the military got, for all along to Clontarf, Glasnevin, and Drumcondra the insurgents held practically undisputed sway.

Another minor position of great importance was the clearing of Stephen's Green by means of a maxim from the "Shelbourne."

The first actual entry of the military in force from an outside area took place on Tuesday evening, when a body of Royal Dublin Fusiliers forced their way into the centre of the city by Cabra Road. The insurgents had placed barricades both on the Park Road and on Cabra Road, near the point at which Charleville Road links up these thoroughfares. Houses overlooking the barricades were occupied by the insurgents, and some brisk fighting took place before the way was cleared for the military advance. A well-directed shell or two demolished the barricades, and within a short time the defenders, under the thunder of artillery, machine guns and rifle-fire, were forced from these positions. There were a couple of civilian casualties resulting from the shrapnel. Attempts by the insurgents to blow up the Cabra Bridge and the bridge crossing the Midland Railway on the North Circular Road beyond Phibsborough Church were unsuccessful.

It was not until Wednesday morning, as we have already seen, that the city realized that an attack in full force was contemplated, and if necessary heavy artillery would be used to dislodge the rebels.

Up to that it had been thought that at the worst gas shells might be dropped upon the enemy strongholds and that the city would be spared: but it early became evident that the disproportion would be too great in the street fighting, which everyone now saw was becoming inevitable.

Accordingly, during the early hours of Wednesday morning a party of six volunteers from Trinity—including both civilians and members of the O.T.C.—went forth to dig holes below the cobbles for the gun-trails. The position was at the Tara Street end of Butt Bridge, and the object, in order to be ready to begin early the shelling of Liberty Hall, which was looked upon as the centre and symbol of the anarchy.

After much difficulty two 18-pounders were brought up and machine guns were placed on the tower of the Fire Station and the Tivoli, and then, when all was ready, the bombardment began. Evidently the rebels had got wind of this intention, however, and though much damage was done, practically no casualties were scored, the rebels getting away through the basement or along the roofs.

The *Helga*, an old police patrol boat belonging to the Fisheries Department, next contributed, though the task was an extremely delicate one, owing to the position of the Custom House and the Railway Bridge, having eventually to retire further down the river and adopt a dropping instead of a direct fire.

For over an hour this naval bombardment continued without eliciting any reply.

It seemed to be generally hoped that the very threat of artillery would be sufficient to cow the rebels, but this was far from being the case. There was a perfect rabbit warren of retreat, and when the troops rushed forward with bayonets fixed and cheering triumphantly, their onrush was unchecked and they found themselves established in—ruins.

The rebel loss was a considerable gain to the troops, for it meant that the military would find themselves connected up with Amiens Street Station; but this was not so easy: they needed more reserves to accomplish a junction, and it was in order to secure these that the "Battle of Mount Street" bridge was fought, an engagement which has been called the "Dardanelles of Dublin," because the place commanded the direct approach of the troops from Kingstown, and I quote my own experience to illustrate the kind of struggle that went on at every entrance to the city.

The "battle" was in every way typical of the kind of fighting which we were destined to witness for the rest of the week, and I was lucky enough to get back from Howth, a journey which I had to cover on foot, just in time to see it from a few minutes after the start.

The Sinn Feiners had got Clanwilliam House—a corner residence— wonderfully barricaded, and the Sherwood Foresters, who had just taken Carisbrook House and Ballsbridge after considerable losses, were now advancing to cross over the canal and so enter the town and relieve the O.T.C. in Trinity.

Clanwilliam House not only dominated the bridge, but also the whole of Northumberland Road.

Along this road the troops had to pass, and they crouched down in long rows of heads—like great khaki caterpillars—in a most terribly exposed order, so that if the rebel shot failed to hit the first head it was bound to hit the second head, provided the rifle was anywhere in the vertical line. For the most part the soldiers were boys in their early twenties, utterly ignorant of the district, with orders to take the town, which was reported in the hands of a body of men whose very name was a mysterious puzzle in pronunciation, and not an enemy in sight, only a mass of civilian spectators up to within fifty yards of them and directly in front, blocking the street— the rebel enemy meanwhile inside private houses to the right and left of the narrow bridgehead, they knew not where.

I arrived on the scene a few minutes after the start of the engagement, but already one could see the poor fellows writhing in agony in the roadway, where the advanced line had been sniped by the terrible leaden bullets of the Sinn Feiners.

For half an hour or so I was a passive spectator, though intensely interested by the sight of a real battle going on under my very eyes at a distance hardly more than that of the gallery from a large music-hall stage; but suddenly I felt a complete change come over me, which I yet fail to explain to myself. The usual cowardice of the spectator seemed to leave me, and I wanted to rush over and help, but I was assured that it would mean instant death to come between the line of combatants—"The Sinn Feiners would fire on anyone, the blackguards." This I refused to believe, and spoke to a Methodist clergyman, who soon shared my views, and together we made our way to Dun's Hospital, where the doctors and nurses in white stood in the doorway. Within a couple of minutes' conversation we had all spontaneously decided to venture under the Red Cross and put it to the test. They gave me the white coat of an ambulance worker, and within five minutes we were all on the bridge together.

Anticipating us all, however, were two little girls of sixteen and seventeen—Kathleen Pierce and Loo Nolan by name—who rushed out of the throng with water in a jug for one of the wounded Tommies who was lying across the bridge bleeding.

A great shout went up from the crowd as they saw this, and both combatants ceased firing, and, after having given the soldiers a drink, they came back amidst the cheers of soldiers, crowd, and Sinn Feiners alike, and they are now known as the bravest colleens in Ireland—God bless them! But little as they realized it, the danger was considerable, and it must ever reflect to the credit of Sir Patrick Dun's Hospital, that scene of the young nurses who flocked out in a body, in spite of the hail of bullets which passed over them and around them on every side. For, try as they would, the two sides could not completely cease fire when every second and every yard was a question of life and death, defeat or victory.

Never shall I forget the experience—the whole staff of doctors gave a hand, together with a clergyman, the Rev. Mr. Hall, of St. John's Voluntary Aid Detachment. I was with Councillor Keogh myself, and poor Hylands, who was afterwards killed, with whom I bore a stretcher, continually bringing in wounded between us. In little over an hour we brought in about seventy poor fellows, who lay about all along the road and canal banks, heavy packs upon their backs.

At last, however, when we had cleared the road of wounded, about dusk, there came a shout from Captain Melleville: "Now, lads, up and all together!" Immediately there was a simultaneous rush across the bridge—a tactic which should have been adopted from the very first. Some dropped, but the numbers were too many for the handful of snipers.

We moved aside to give them room, and the next moment the bombers were in the garden of Clanwilliam House—one poor fellow falling and blowing the top of his head off at the gate with his own grenade.

There was a "Crash! crash! crash!" as the windows burst with the concussion, and within a few seconds the sky was lit up with the flare of the burning houses and the air rent with the screams of the Sinn Feiners as they faced cold steel. It was a ghastly scene!

The smell of roasting flesh was still around the blazing buildings at ten o'clock, when we brought in the last of the dead—some of them mere boys of thirteen—and laid them out in dread rows like a Raemaeker cartoon.

One lad of twelve whom I carried in I afterwards interrogated as to why he was out in such an exposed position. He wanted to give a poor Tommy a drink, and got sniped as he was preparing to get down to the water of the canal.

The Dardanelles had been forced, however, and the highway into Dublin secured.

All Wednesday night the whole town was kept awake by the snipers, who now became one of the main features of the turmoil; they seemed to be everywhere, but it was almost impossible to locate them.

Troops lined the streets in the direction of Merrion and Fitzwilliam Squares, and were picked off from windows and roofs all night in the most bewildering fashion, while the slum courts in the centre of the large blocks of buildings re-echoed with the sharp click of the old rebel mausers, till the military were tempted to fire on any strange figure looming up in the distance.

During the night several transports had arrived, we now heard, and the troops soon began to land in force.

All Thursday I spent with the Red Cross at Sir Patrick Dun's, which was crowded with casualties, poor fellows! one raving and asking "Is the school taken?—is the school taken?": for this point had been the strategic point in the Battle of Mount Street Bridge. It was pathetic.

All day long the troops arrived, but whenever crossing the side streets, which were slums honeycombed with snipers, they would have to "double" and rush across in single file; but each time one or two were picked off by the deadly snipers, all firing from cover, with thick lead bullets that spread and made dreadful wounds—some, inches wide. In the yard the Raemaeker picture of the dead soldiers—Sinn Feiners—was broader by some half-dozen: for several had died of wounds during the night. The small boy who had been sniped while trying to get the soldiers a drink lay stiff now, and my mind went back to the scene of the night before as I made a little space of a couple of yards in the corner of the crowded ward, with everyone lying on the floor, while the good priest anointed him just before he died.

All day long and all around there was a perfect hail of bullets from the snipers, some going right through the hospital grounds from Boland's bakery, which, sandbagged and loopholed, was filled with Sinn Feiners. It was a terrible fight, for of course it was next to impossible for the soldiers to distinguish them, being all in civilian clothes so that they just had to doff their bandoliers and they could go about from house to house in safety. Sometimes they did this purposely, having arms in several places. Hence the order had to go out that all civilians would have to stay indoors, and after that all suspicious characters were shot at, with the terrible result that innocent civilians were killed on all sides.

Accordingly, while on our way to pick up a body I went with one of the stretcher-bearers and a priest and a parson to warn them to keep indoors.

One poor fellow we brought in, shot through the breast, was apparently a civilian, but on examination we found on him a curious document, undoubtedly proving him a Sinn Feiner.

The story of this document, which was perhaps the final decisive factor that precipitated the rising, is perhaps best told in the words of the Royal Commission:—

> On the 19th of April a special meeting of the Dublin Corporation was held at the Mansion House to discuss the police rate. Alderman Thomas Kelly, in the course of a speech attacking Mr. Justice Kenny (who had alluded at the opening of his Commission to the state of disorder in Dublin and had urged military action), made a statement to the effect that he had received that morning from the editor of *New Ireland* a circular which he would read. It was from a man named Little, *New Ireland* Office, 13, Fleet Street, Dublin, April 16, 1916, and ran:—
>
> "The following precautionary measures have been sanctioned by the Irish Office on the recommendation of the General Officer Commanding the Forces in Ireland. All preparations will be made to put these measures in force immediately on receipt of an Order issued from the

Chief Secretary's Office, Dublin Castle, and signed by the Under Secretary and the General Officer Commanding the Forces in Ireland. First, the following persons to be placed under arrest:—All members of the Sinn Fein National Council, the Central Executive Irish Sinn Fein Volunteers, General Council Irish Sinn Fein Volunteers, County Board Irish Sinn Fein Volunteers, Executive Committee National Volunteers, Coisde Gnota Committee Gaelic League. See List A 3 and 4 and supplementary list A 2.... Dublin Metropolitan Police and Royal Irish Constabulary Forces in Dublin City will be confined to barracks under the direction of the Competent Military Authority. An order will be issued to inhabitants of city to remain in their houses until such time as the Competent Military Authority may otherwise direct or permit. Pickets chosen from units of Territorial Forces will be placed at all points marked on maps 3 and 4. Accompanying mounted patrols will continuously visit all points and report every hour. The following premises will be occupied by adequate forces, and all necessary measures used without need of reference to headquarters; after which followed a list.

"Alderman Kelly, in continuing, said that the document was evidently genuine, and that he had done a public service in drawing attention to it, in order to prevent these military operations being carried on in a city which he declared was under God the most peaceable in Europe.

"This document was an entire fabrication. Copies of it found since the outbreak are shown by identification of type to have been printed at Liberty Hall, the headquarters of the Citizen Army. It is not known who was the author of this invention, or whether Mr. Little was in any way responsible for it. Many copies of this forged document were printed and distributed, and it was widely considered by the people to be genuine, and no doubt led to the belief by the members of the Irish Volunteers and Citizen Army that they would shortly be disarmed. This undoubtedly became one of the proximate causes of the outbreak."

All Thursday seems to have been devoted principally to the bringing in of reinforcements, which, by this time, were pouring in from England.

Instead of using them for isolated attacks on the different strongholds, they appear to have been concentrated as an ever-narrowing cordon around the central position of the rebels at the Post Office.

Hence, by Thursday evening the tables had been completely turned upon the rebels, and instead of dominating the city, the city on every side hemmed them in; and the Law Courts, the College of Surgeons, Jacobs's biscuit factory and Boland's bakery, though amply supplied with food and ammunition, had been all practically isolated one from another—in the last-named place the rebels forced the bakers, at the point of the bayonet, to continue making bread.

The military were also in possession of Brunswick Street, and portions of Talbot Street and North Earl Street, while from D'Olier Street a fusillade swept O'Connell Bridge, and from T.C.D. a 9-pounder began to batter down Kelly's corner house and send shells along Bachelors' Walk.

Everybody now expected the collapse of the rebels, who were being captured on all sides, and crowds of British pressmen, with special facilities for the edification of neutral countries, began to arrive.

Certainly never had journalists ever had such a finale to send flashing along the wires; for a cordon of soldiers completely encircled the city on every side, and grew gradually tighter and tighter around the Post Office, the heart of the rebel position. From all sides shells now began to drop into Sackville Street, and we knew that it was the beginning of the end.

That end was in every way as dramatic as the beginning—a melodrama worthy of the Lyceum at its best—and for thirty hours, as the artillery thundered, the sky was one huge blaze of flame, which, at one time, threatened to engulf the whole northern centre of the city in a sea of fire.

Driven from Kelly's corner, which commanded the left entrance to Sackville Street, the insurgents still held Hopkins's corner on the other side, and on this the artillery next concentrated not only high explosive shells but incendiary bombs as well, and the whole place became a mass of blazing ruins, the flames leaping across Lower Abbey Street like a prairie fire.

Whether this was intentional or inevitable, one thing was certain, and that was that nothing could stand up against it—it meant utter annihilation as far as human lives were concerned, absolute ruination as far as material property.

That strong measures had been found necessary, however, had been proved by the appointment of a military dictator in General Sir John Maxwell, with plenary powers, and the announcement of Mr. Asquith in the House that the situation had still serious features, and that there seemed to be indications of the movement spreading to other parts of the country, especially the West.

Yet one thing must have been particularly pleasing to announce, and that was the total isolation of the movement as a political campaign, both Sir Edward Carson and Mr. John Redmond disclaiming all responsibility, while in Drogheda the National Volunteers, according to a telegram from the Viceroy, actually turned out to assist the military.

This background of peace only served to intensify the catastrophe which became known as the Sack of Sackville Street, and it is probable that only the gap made by the fire which occurred on Tuesday afternoon at Lawrence's bazaar saved the northern portion of the city.

It was under cover of the blazing buildings that the troops advanced upon the central position of the Sinn Feiners, one of the pickets being inside Clery's while the embers beneath his feet were still red, as I was told: but it was not until Saturday morning that the actual final shelling and capture of the place was begun.

For this purpose only light shells, happily, were used, and some incendiary bombs, which soon set fire to the roof of the beautiful historic landmark.

It was expected that at least a thousand of the rebels were entrapped, but it was later found out that during the week they had made a complete tunnel right back as far as Arnot's Stores, blasting their way with the aid of dynamite, in the use of which they seem to have been coached by a Berlin expert, who was afterwards captured.

The last struggles of the rebels have been variously described, but they seem rather early to have made an attempt in force to evacuate the building from the back, and some hundred and fifty are described as taking part in the stampede, which was turned into a rout by the machine guns of the military.

A single shell which exploded right in the barricade in front of the Coliseum building, which faces a side street, had the effect not only of closing it by the wreckage of the two corner buildings, but also of burying one of the rebel leaders.

Everyone then expected that the place would be taken at the point of the bayonet and a terrible hand-to-hand struggle ensue, as the troops would thrust the despairing rebels back into the fortress, which was rapidly turning into a furnace, when suddenly the order was given to cease fire, and for fully three hours there was a mysterious silence.

Had the place been taken, had the men surrendered, or was it only a truce, as one rumour had it, in order to enable the city to get in foodstuffs?—for the food problem had by this time become most acute in several of the isolated districts.

It proved to be an armistice, during which terms of formal surrender were concluded with the insurgent leaders, and a short while after four, Sackville Street beheld the sight of all that were left of them, the gallant but misguided six hundred, marching into captivity.

"It is a sight I shall never forget," said one eye-witness who beheld the surrender from a window in the Gresham Hotel. "That thin, short line of no more than a hundred men at most, some in the green uniform of the Volunteers, some in the plainer equipment of Larkin's Citizen Army, some looking like ordinary civilians, some again mere lads of fifteen, not a few wounded and bandaged, the whole melancholy procession threading its way through long lines of khaki soldiers—but downhearted? No; and as they passed, I heard just for a couple of seconds the subdued strains of that scaffold-song of many an Irishman before them—'God save Ireland'—waft up to me.

"Roughs, dockers, labourers, shop-assistants—all kinds and conditions of men, even the lowest class in the city—yet all exactly the same in the look of defiance which will haunt me to my dying day.

"Whatever they were, these men were no cowards—and even the soldiers admitted this readily; they had shown courage of the finest type, worthy of a nobler cause; and had they been man for man at the front and accomplished what they had accomplished in the face of such odds, the whole Empire would have been proud of them—the whole world ringing with their praise; for, as a soldier prisoner afterwards said, 'Not even the hell of Loos or Neuve Chapelle was like the hell of those last hours in the General Post Office.'

"Instead of that, they were doomed to the double stigma of failure in accomplishment and futility in aim—but every Irish heart went out to them, for all that, for were they not our own flesh and blood after all?

"At either end a lad carried an improvised white flag of truce—at their head, Pearse in full uniform, with sword across one arm in regular surrender fashion. For a moment the young British officer in command seemed perplexed at the solemnity of the procession and at the correctness and courtesy of the rebel leader; and he hesitatingly accepted the sword from his hands.

"The next moment the spell was broken: the man was a captive criminal, and with two officers, each with a loaded revolver pointing at his head, the chief and his gallant band disappeared from my view."

CHAPTER THE FOURTH

SURRENDER—COLLAPSE

Late on that fateful Saturday evening upon which the Post Office fell, the Royal Irish Constabulary were posting in all parts of the country the following note signed by Commander P. H. Pearse.

"In order to prevent further slaughter," it ran, "of unarmed people, and in the hope of saving the lives of our followers, now surrounded and hopelessly outnumbered, members of the Provisional Government present at headquarters have agreed to unconditional surrender, and the commanders of all units of the Republican forces will order their followers to lay down their arms."

Yet so confident were the rebels of success in some of the besieged fortresses that they positively refused to believe that their commanders had given in: moreover, the difficulty of obtaining access to some of the insurgents also tended to prolong the conflict, especially in the more outlying districts, and so the struggle went on.

In some cases the rebels, expecting no mercy, preferred to die fighting, and it was only by the interference of the clergy that further destruction and desolation was avoided.

Jacobs's factory, for example—second only to Guinness's Brewery in size, and occupied at first by some 1,500 rebels, who had taken possession while the workers were on holiday—put up a strenuous fight, and though it was by now surrounded by the military, the men, firmly protected and encouraged by the feeling that headquarters depended upon them, refused all offers to surrender.

Several priests had previously made the attempt to influence them, but had been quietly and courteously refused, and only succeeded eventually about 4 p.m. on Sunday, when the Volunteers finally evacuated the premises.

The majority of the exits had by Sunday become occupied by the military, who had gradually turned the place into a death-trap, and from this the rebels were saved by a somewhat picturesque climax.

A well-known Carmelite monk from Whitefriars Street suddenly made his way through the crowd of spectators and signalled to the insurgents, whereupon one of the sandbagged windows was dismantled and, amid a universal cheer from the crowd, the venerable peacemaker was hoisted up into the fortress.

A short while later his efforts were seen to have succeeded, for the garrison surrendered.

At the Four Courts a priest was likewise instrumental in bringing about the surrender.

The place had been strongly barricaded and provisioned, and would, no doubt, have suffered the same fate as the Post Office had the struggle continued, but for this intervention and the desire on the part of the authorities no doubt to save the Record Office at all costs. Such a loss would, of course, have been far more serious than that of the G.P.O., for in some cases all kinds of documents had been used for the purposes of defence, at one particular spot a whole barricade having been constructed of wills alone.

Father Columbus, O.S.F.C., who was at the time attending to the wounded and dying, saw a girl waving a large white sheet from the building, and we immediately proceeded to inform the military authorities, who were still pounding away at the building with maxims, of the intention of the insurgents to surrender.

An officer was dispatched, and to him Commander Daly, of the Republican Army, rendered unconditional surrender on behalf of the besieged.

Another dramatic surrender on Sunday was that of the College of Surgeons, where the rebels had been making a stout resistance, under the personal command of the celebrated Countess Markievicz.

The green flag which had floated there throughout the week in spite of shot and shell was suddenly lowered, and one of the rebels was seen to climb on the parapet and tie a white scarf, quaintly enough, on to the arm of the central statue, which stood out against the skyline, instead of the flagstaff.

A few seconds later this formal announcement of surrender was followed by the order to "cease fire," and a detachment of soldiers was sent to that side of Stephen's Green.

As they approached, the Countess, who was dressed in a complete outfit of the green uniform of the Irish Volunteers, including green boots and green cock's feathers, something like those on the Italian bersaglieri, emerged from the central doorway. She was closely followed by an attendant carrying a white flag and some sixty to eighty of the defenders.

Solemnly they advanced towards the English officer, and then the Countess, taking off her bandolier and sword, was seen to kiss them reverently and hand them over in the most touching manner—not a little to the perplexity of the young officer.

Dr. Myles Keogh, who, in company with others, acted so bravely in rescuing the wounded, tells of the actual incident of the surrender of De Valera, near Ringsend. Dr. Keogh was on Sunday returning at one o'clock from Glasnevin Cemetery on a hearse, which, under the Red Cross, had left a number of dead for burial, and when opposite Sir Patrick Dun's Hospital a voice hailed him. Two men had come out of the Poor Law Dispensary opposite, in which the Sinn Feiners were installed. So covered with dust were they that he thought both were in khaki. One was a military cadet who had been captured by the Sinn Feiners, the other was the Sinn Fein leader De Valera. "Hullo!" cried De Valera. "Who are you?" replied Dr. Keogh. The response was, "I am De Valera," from one, and from the other it was: "I am a prisoner for the past five days. They want to surrender." Dr. Keogh replied that Sir Arthur Ball, who was in the hospital, would make arrangements. Then the military came up, and after some preliminaries the Sinn Feiners were marched out of the dispensary and conveyed to Lower Mount Street. The hopelessness of the Sinn Feiners was exemplified in some remarks dropped by De Valera. "Shoot me," he said, "if you will, but arrange for my men." Then he added, walking up and down: "If only the people had come out with knives and forks."

I saw Dr. Keogh immediately after this, and he told me that De Valera had complained bitterly that the "English" had continuously violated the white flag and Red Cross, but we could testify to the falsity of this by our own experience, the whole staff having time after time complained that shots appeared to go right across the hospital—and, in point of fact, the right wing of "Elpis" Hospital is simply peppered with bullets—in fact, the wounded Tommies "sunning" themselves on the hospital roof of Dun's had been deliberately fired at till they went down, though I must admit that in this case the Sinn Feiners could hardly have been able to make the distinction required of them. A short while later I saw the professor himself—a tall man, hatless and in the green uniform of the Volunteers—pass along Mount Street with a lad with a white flag, going to point out the positions of the snipers from the factory.

For a moment the soldiers thought he was about to "betray" his pals to save his own life, and, I was glad to notice, instinctively looked with contempt upon him; but the truth of the general order having gone out to surrender soon became known, and as the line of captives marched by the soldiers for the first time got a real look at these men who had, so to speak, staggered the Empire.

Weak, poor, ragged—some cripples; one, his whole face a mass of bandages—I never saw a more reckless or determined body of men in my life, and they contrasted strangely with the placid demeanour of their conquerors. Each marched with a certain lightness of tread—greybeards who no doubt remembered the days of the Famine and boys born since the Boer War; and as they stood there, their hands aloft, between the lines of khaki, not one face flinched. Here and there, however, one could see the older men shaking hands with the younger, muttering, "It isn't the first time we've suffered. But it's all for dear old Ireland," or wishing each other good-bye. That was pathetic to a degree that, I know for a fact, moved some of the English officers themselves.

Suddenly a car came dashing up at full speed. Some turned their heads instinctively, and as they did so noticed that in addition to four khaki uniforms there were two green figures with eyes bandaged.

In an instant the captives had recognized their leaders, themselves also going—God only knew to what punishment, and at once such a cheer went up that the whole street echoed again.

It only needed "God save Ireland" to have completed the drama, but they knew they would be stopped if they began, and, instead, one of them cried out "Are we downhearted?" and immediately every voice, clear and resonant, answered in one ringing "No!"

"If it had not been for the women and children, we should be fighting you still," was the reply of one Sinn Feiner to a soldier; and when asked why they were fighting, another man answered, "We have our orders as well as you—we're both soldiers and fight when our country demands"; while yet a third ventured defiantly, "You've won this time, but next time when you're fighting, our children will win."

Dramatic was no word for the situation, and as I gazed at them there—now no more than a dread convict roll—I pictured the wretched tenements from which most must have come—the worst slums in Europe, by common consent of all Commissions—and asked myself the question what chance or reason they had ever had in life to love either their country or the Empire; and then the picture of the long years of penal servitude, such as John Mitchel had endured for Ireland, arose before my mind, but I consoled myself with the thought, "At least England will understand what caused these men to turn despairingly to revolution," and the words of Mr. Asquith consoled me as I thought of the terrible wholesale vengeance a Prussian officer would take—for had he not said that England had sent the General in whose discretion she had more complete confidence than any other?—but I stopped thinking: it was all too sad: after all, England was surely not going to treat them like the Huns would.

I heard one young Lancashire Tommy say: "The poor beggars! They only obeyed the word of command, and they fought like heroes," but he was cut short by an English officer with an Oxford drawl: "Damn sympathizing with the swine! I'd shoot all these Irish rebels down like rats—every one of them—if I had my way."

The words struck me forcibly at the time, for I knew that it only needed this to make martyrs of every one of them.

"England has learnt how fatal that mistake has been," I replied. "We're surely not going to set Ireland back a hundred years by such a pogrom as followed '98...."

Meanwhile, though in Dublin we knew very little, the movement in the provinces had long since been crushed: indeed, it never appears to have had much chance of success.

It was said that some delay or interruption in the sending of the signal message was the cause. Others say that the South had orders to await the landing of arms from the German cruiser which brought over Sir Roger Casement, and which was sunk on April 21st—which seems the more probable.

This news, however, seems, for mysterious reasons, to have been kept from the general public, for it was not till the Monday evening, at 10.23, that this announcement was made, and, reaching Ireland on the morrow of the announcement of the triumph of the Republic in the capital, must have shown the waverers that the rising was bound to end in a fiasco—a fact which they possibly realized better than the men in Dublin, who to the very end seem to have expected something to turn up.

It was generally expected that Cork would rise *en masse*, for the Sinn Feiners had been organizing the city and county for upwards of three years—in most cases the gradually increasing forces being drilled by ex-soldiers privately, so that when they eventually appeared publicly on parade and in full uniform, marching through the streets in a body four deep, with rifles on their shoulders, everyone realized that the movement had amply justified itself.

Every Sunday, public parades showed a growing strength that at times alarmed the authorities to no little degree.

The mass demonstration at Limerick about a year ago still further revealed their strength, and from that moment to the fateful Easter week the organization, already considerable in point of numbers, perfected itself by the addition of ammunition, uniforms, equipment, and financial aid.

Everybody expected that there would be some sort of ructions between the Volunteers and the military on last St. Patrick's Day, when it was announced that the Sinn Feiners would parade fully armed and with a real maxim gun, but luckily nothing happened.

The next crisis was seen to approach in Holy Week, when large numbers of strangers were noticed to be arriving daily from every part of the country and putting up at lodging-houses.

The strangers were next noticed to be paying continual visits to the Sinn Fein headquarters in Shears Street, extensive premises that were once a hospital.

On the outbreak in Dublin the whole place was put into a state of expectant siege, with passwords and guards, much in the same way as at the G.P.O. in the capital, but no outbreak occurred.

On the Wednesday the Lord Mayor and the Bishop of Cork were able to obtain an interview with the leaders, and as a result of the conference a temporary sort of truce was arranged, which was never really broken, though at times it was a matter of touch and go.

That it would have been serious cannot be doubted, for they claimed no less than six hundred men at headquarters, and anything up from a thousand within the boundaries of the city, to say nothing of the surrounding districts, which were anything but favourable either to John Redmond or William O'Brien.

Now, the inner history of the negotiation, which was later made public in a letter from the Assistant-Bishop of Cork to the *Freeman's Journal,* is of supreme importance for two reasons.

In the first place, it explains the kind of influences which were at work all over the country to prevent the spread of the outbreak by the better-disposed and more sober-minded of the population.

In the second place, by revealing the psychology of some of the provincial leaders it goes not a little to establish my theory that even as late as Monday night something might have been done had the leaders of the "Republic"— which it must never be forgotten had always been a "provisional" term— been approached by the best spirits in Ireland herself, instead of immediately launching an army corps of troops and a naval detachment bald-headed on to the guns of the Volunteers, who could never have expected to bring off a victory in the real sense of the term, and who were only anxious to offer themselves as a willing holocaust to the Spirit of Nationality they thought was dying fast because it had merged itself into the Spirit of Empire.

As to Kerry, it was looked upon as being "rotten" with Sinn Fein, and had there been a rising, these men would undoubtedly have marched to the help of their Cork brethren.

The theory of the Kerry correspondent of the *Times* is that the South was awaiting the advent of Sir Roger Casement, who was to have invaded Ireland with a fleet of battle cruisers and an army of 40,000 men, but this ended in as complete a fiasco as the landing of Napper Tandy at Rutland or Wolf Tone in Lough Swilly in 1798.

The rising, however, was not strictly speaking dependent on Sir Roger Casement at all: indeed, as afterwards appeared, he had himself tried to stop the rising by saying that German help had failed.

It appears, moreover, that in Dublin the heads of the Irish Volunteers had long since come under the strong personal influence of the heads of the Citizen Army, and it was these latter who forced the pace; and in admitting this, one is forced to conclude that the rising was as much socialistic and economic as national. This, too, would explain why it was almost entirely confined to Dublin. For only in about three or four other places in Ireland were there risings of any note, and even these were comparatively unimportant: though, of course, there is no knowing to what proportions they might not have swelled had the risings in Kerry and Cork been carried out.

The Volunteers of Swords, for example, who only began activities about seven o'clock on the Wednesday morning, commenced by a capture of the barracks and post office, both of which were in their possession by about 8.30.

Their *coup* was a minor replica of the Dublin affray. Two of their leaders, a doctor and a school-teacher, rode up in a motor-car as if paying a harmless call, and then suddenly produced revolvers and covered the sergeant, who was standing at the door, saying at the same time: "We want no trouble, but the arms and ammunition you have in the barracks."

At the same moment about fifty other Volunteers closed in from behind, with the result that the three unfortunate policemen could do nothing but surrender, and the booty was distributed amongst the unarmed Volunteers, and whatever was over stored for any recruits the valour of this exploit might bring to the new colours.

The door of the post office was next charged at by three of the strongest of the Volunteers, but being ajar, was consequently entered in the most undignified way by the invaders, who fell head-over-heels into the place, which was a couple of feet below the street-level—luckily for themselves, their rifles not going off.

The telegraphic wires and apparatus were then broken up, and then, proceeding in the direction of Donabate, the railway bridge at Rodgerstown was blown up, cutting off Dublin.

Meanwhile, information had reached Malahide, and there the constabulary at once proceeded to entrench themselves along the railway, in order to protect the important bridge there; but the insurgents did not venture, having already found the contingent that was engaged in a deadly encounter with the Meath police at Ashbourne, towards the end of the week, encamping between Fieldstown and Kilsallaghan.

Here, early on Sunday morning, they were surprised to receive a copy of the proclamation issued by P. H. Pearse, advising them to surrender unconditionally. So surprised in fact were they, that they determined to keep "the ambassador of peace" as a hostage until they verified the astounding news for themselves, one of their leaders motoring up to Dublin with the Chief Constable. On their return, of course, with the news confirmed, there was nothing to do but surrender, and this they accordingly did—their only stipulation being that they should be spared the humiliation of going back through Swords, where most of them lived.

The rising at Enniscorthy at one time threatened to be a more serious affair, though it only began on the Thursday, when the Athenæum, one of the principal buildings of the town, was seized and turned into a headquarters by the insurgent staff.

Several hundreds of Sinn Feiners now assembled outside, and several dozen motor-cars which had been "commandeered," together with stores of petrol and food, and the men were all served out with ammunition, while amidst huge enthusiasm the green, white, and orange Republican flag was hoisted over the building.

Afterwards railway lines and telegraphs were destroyed by a special force and the town methodically taken over, all business houses and licensed premises being closed, with the exception of the gasworks and the bakeries, where the employees were compelled to perform their public duties in the name of the Commonwealth.

The R.I.C. barracks alone held out, being well supplied with ammunition, but the police there were powerless to interfere, having to stand a sort of siege day after day.

Enniscorthy Castle, which commands the town, was taken from Mr. Henry Roche, J.P. All food and arms and vehicles throughout the town were commandeered. But there was no looting, a considerable body of young men having been formed into a species of Republican police—an organization which would have saved the Dublin rising half its horrors.

The ladies of the "Cumann na Ban" next turned the top story of the Athenæum into an improvised hospital, and here were brought the wounded in the attack on the constabulary barracks, which lasted all Thursday and part of Friday.

Friday was spent in preparation and expectation—the news of the collapse of the revolt in Dublin not having yet reached them—and on Saturday a motor expedition to Ferns resulted in the capture of the post office and barracks.

As food had now become scarce, shops were only allowed to sell limited quantities, and as the situation was becoming dangerous, with the expected advent of the military, pickets were placed at street corners, and these insisted on the civilian population keeping within doors.

Another strange, though by no means uncommon, sight was whole rows of Volunteers going up to the Cathedral for confession, and on the Sunday attending Mass.

The clergy, while not refusing them the consolations of religion, however, in no way encouraged them in their illusion of success, for on the Sunday morning a party of citizens from Arklow brought a priest under cover of the white flag to announce to the rebels the collapse of the rising in Dublin.

A deputation of the town was then sent to Wexford to interview the military there, who confirmed the news; but, as elsewhere, even this did not satisfy them, and they refused to surrender the town of Enniscorthy until their leaders had seen Dublin's disaster with their own eyes.

Even then the "commanders" wanted to hold out, and, as the *Daily Sketch* correspondent pointed out, it was only when the chief citizens themselves made the petition that the Volunteers at last consented.

Indeed, it would have been hard to conceive how they could logically have insisted on defending the town, which refused to acknowledge them; and the rebels, in justice be it said of them, were nothing if not logical—even if only the logic of madmen. If Ireland refused to look upon them as saviours, then they were not going to play the part of tyrants; and it seems to me that if the civil authorities of Dublin had taken up this stand on the Tuesday morning, the whole thing might have fizzled off without a single further military casualty.

On Monday therefore—to continue the story of the Enniscorthy rising— the rebels surrendered unconditionally to Colonel French, who entered the town at the head of two thousand military.

At Wexford the situation was saved, as at Drogheda, by the assistance of the National Volunteers, who, under Colonel Jameson Davis, turned out to assist the police, the Lord Mayor and six hundred of the chief citizens enrolling themselves also as special constables.

In Galway rebellion has always been in the blood. It was from Athenry, eleven miles east of Galway, that the "Invincibles," who were responsible for the Phœnix Park murders, came; and an interesting account was given of the rising which now took place at Athenry by one of the special correspondents of the Press, Mr. Hugh Martin.

According to this account the central figure was a "Captain" Mellows, who, deported a month before from Ireland, had managed to make his escape from England, and avoiding detection by the constabulary under the disguise of a priest, suddenly turned up at the psychological moment a few days before the outbreak of the rising in Dublin.

The Town Hall of Athenry, on Sunday and Monday, seemed to have aroused a certain amount of suspicion—it was suspected of being a centre of illegal munition making—but it was not till the Tuesday, thirty-six hours after the seizure of the Dublin Post Office, that it suddenly revealed itself in its true colours, when "Captain" Mellows unexpectedly appeared in the green uniform of an Irish Volunteer and proclaimed the establishment of an Irish Republic to a body of some five hundred Volunteers, two-thirds of whom were armed with rifles and the rest with shot-guns and pikes.

Overcoming the local police, they proceeded to take one of the Irish Board of Agriculture's model farms about three-quarters of a mile from Athenry, and having captured the place and appropriated all money, settled for the night.

The next day, after a vain attempt by the police to dislodge them, they marched, several hundreds strong, with a whole train of wagons and carts filled with food of every description, towards Loughrea, where they captured Lady Ardilaun's seat, Moyode Castle, from the lonely caretaker, John Shackleton, and his pretty eighteen-year-old daughter Maisie.

A curious figure now appeared in the person of Father Feeny, who, according to Hugh Martin, appears to have exercised as much control over the men as the "Captain" himself.

His influence seems to have been on the whole for good, for the account describes him as hearing the men's confessions and insisting that the fifteen to twenty young colleens who were one of the most curious features of the local rising, marching beside the men and doing all their cooking, should be separately accommodated in the castle at night.

Some isolated R.I.C. men who happened to fall into their hands were treated as prisoners, but when on the Thursday afternoon the police from Athenry made an attack, they were chased with motor-cars for a distance of about four miles back to Athenry, where the forces of the Crown only just managed to get into their barracks in the nick of time.

The next day—Friday—saw the positions reversed, and news reached the rebels that troops and artillery were on their way from Loughrea, some six miles' distance, and it was the rebels' turn to turn tail, scattering as they went to right and left, in spite of every effort of "Captain" Mellows to encourage them with stories of the coming invasion by Germany.

Some made for the hills, others tried to get back to their homes, but most were seized by the Belfast police, in cars driven by Ulster Volunteers, and those who did get back had to face not only the taunt of ignominious defeat but the anger of the Redmondites, who now foresaw the possibilities of a retribution quite out of all proportion to the chances they had ever had of success.

Indeed, that seems to have been the general result of the collapse of the rebellion all over Ireland; and though at first it apparently tended to weaken the hands of the Irish Constitutional leader—who, when the news came to him, must have felt as he had on that famous occasion when, as a young man, five minutes before having to make a great speech near Manchester, he was handed the news of the Phœnix Park murders—on the whole it really considerably strengthened his position, much in the same way as the revolt of De Wet brought out the loyalty of General Botha.

Botha, indeed, was one of the very first to see the similarity of the two cases, and wired at once to Redmond, though it can of course only be taken as a very superficial verdict of the South African Premier on the real grievances underlying the movement, since he could hardly be expected to understand Sinn Fein, much less those subtle provocations which eventually counselled the mad appeal to Germany; for there can be little doubt but that, if Castle rule had prevailed in Pretoria as it still does in Dublin, South Africa would long since have been a consenting party to German occupation.

This, however, was only one of the subtler aspects of the rising which hardly found its way across the Channel, and consequently could scarcely be expected to appeal to a colonial who was not an Irishman himself.

As the collapse became more general, however, it became more and more evident to intelligent statesmen that it was more a hatred of Castle rule than a love of German rule that had been at the bottom of it all, and that it had been, in spite of the bluster of foreign alliance, more an armed protest against a domestic state of affairs than a real attempt to sever the Imperial link; nevertheless, the latter idea still survived in the minds of the military authorities, who could see in it nothing else, with the disastrous results that only became evident in the aftermath.

CHAPTER THE FIFTH

AFTERMATH

The surrender and collapse of the abortive rising was no sooner over than the whole affair took an entirely new aspect and passed through a completely new phase when it came to deciding what should be thought of the incident and what should be done to the prisoners.

It called for the utmost delicacy of handling on all sides, but this is just what it did not get, and at once there was a complete revulsion of feeling for the Sinn Feiners which, had it come before the rising, might have enabled them to sweep everything before them.

The psychological change is curious as a study in Irish politics.

The first announcement of the rising was so sudden that it took all but those immediately concerned entirely by surprise, and after a moment of almost speechless amazement the movement was promptly denounced by every moderate man in Ireland.

To the Nationalists it appeared at first as if it were the tearing asunder of the Home Rule Bill and the ruination of the constitutional cause for ever. Consequently their attitude was, from their own point of view, perfectly correct, viz. unqualified denunciation. But as further details came along and their opponents in England began to make capital out of it, the case became different. The cry went up that it was want of strength on the part of Mr. Birrell, the Chief Secretary, who could do nothing but resign under the circumstances; and so pained was he that he even went to the length of what was called a confession of guilt: but his weakness had really been great strength—for any weakling can be strong enough to sign an order for wholesale slaughter if he "damns the consequences."

True, there could be no minimizing of the event either in the matter of casualties or damage done.

A fortnight previous and Ireland was still the "one bright spot" and Sackville Street one of the finest thoroughfares in the kingdom, but during those momentous days the capital had been for the greater part of a week almost entirely in the hands of the rebels; a Republican flag had taken the place of the English Jack, which had floated over it for seven continuous centuries, and now Dublin lay a heap of crumbling buildings, whose smoking ruins looked like the track of the Huns—it might now be called Ypres-on-the-Liffey.

The loss of life, too, had been tremendous, but the military casualties were out of all proportion to those of the rebels, in some cases the skirmishes representing a proportion of ten, and even twenty, to one. The casualties, in fact, were as high as many a Boer War battle, and amounted to three hundred killed and over a thousand wounded, of which nearly two hundred were civilians. They included over sixty officers and about four hundred rank and file. The Royal Irish Constabulary lost two killed and thirty-five wounded; the Dublin Metropolitan Police six; the Royal Navy three; and the Loyal Volunteers sixteen. With regard to the Sinn Feiners no figures are available, but they must have been considerably less than a quarter of these—perhaps even under.

The circumstances under which the troops and police suffered, however, were such that the severest measures were adopted by General Sir John Maxwell, who issued the following statement with regard to the action of the courts martial:—

"In view of the gravity of the rebellion and its connection with German intrigue propaganda, and in view of the great loss of life and destruction of property resulting therefrom, the General Officer Commanding-in-Chief has found it imperative to inflict the most severe sentences on the known organizers of this detestable rising and on those commanders who took an active part in the actual fighting which occurred. It is hoped that these examples will be sufficient to act as a deterrent to intriguers and to bring home to them that the murder of His Majesty's liege subjects or other acts calculated to imperil the safety of the realm will not be tolerated."

The military authorities have been blamed for the excessive rigour with which these orders were carried out, especially for the use of shells, but it may be questioned how far this did not arise purely from the nature of the situation.

Certainly the rebels were at a disadvantage, and consequently won a certain amount of sympathy, yet only a day before that sympathy was entirely with the unfortunate military; but eventually a point was reached when, instead of the military retrieving the situation lost by the weakness of the politicians, it became a question whether they were not undoing a good deal that it had taken a great deal of hard work upon the part of the politicians to build up.

Now this is no idle theory, but the only possible explanation of a series of changes that ensued.

When the news of the rising was first announced to John Redmond, he made a dignified if not too diplomatic reply, in which he expressed despair about the situation and utter disgust about the culprits.

The next official utterance was the somewhat ponderous manifesto of the Irish Party—interesting as an historical summary of Ireland's real attitude to the Empire, but lacking a grip of the actual psychological drama of the situation.

The same may be said of the Irish leader's first appeal for clemency in the treatment of the prisoners.

It was in the shape of a question asked of Mr. Asquith as to whether he was aware that the continuance of military executions in Ireland had caused rapidly increasing bitterness and exasperation among large sections of the population who had no sympathy with the rising, and whether it might not be better to follow the precedent set up by General Botha in South Africa, where only one had been executed and the rest exceedingly leniently treated, and stop the executions forthwith.

The Premier's reply was a curt refusal, phrased in the terms of an absolute confidence in the discretion of the military authorities.

Unfortunately that "discretion" was exercised in such a manner as at once to place its victims in the same category as Emmet, Wolf Tone, and the Manchester Martyrs. In a word, to use the words of an English critic, "It gave the Sinn Feiners the real victory, for it was looked upon as the verification of all that they had feared and prophesied, and for which they had, until that point, been looked upon as fools and scaremongers."

Looking back over the situation at this critical juncture, it may well be doubted whether it was altogether wise to carry out any sentences into execution, and the Bishop of Limerick referred very pointedly to the example of a very similar situation in the case of the Jameson raid, when the leniency of the Boer Republicans towards the raiders avoided war with England.

Technically, of course, the two were exactly parallel—by all the laws of sovereignty a rebel deserves instant death; but it became a question of diplomacy as well—a point which seems to have been lost in the clash of battle.

In other words, had time allowed—and of course there was no knowing what effect the resistance of Dublin might have on the country—it may be a moot point whether it might not have been advisable to separate the two questions of the sentence of death and the actual executions, and one can well imagine the conciliatory effect of a Royal Act of Clemency in the event of maturer consideration making it advisable to commute those sentences.

Thus Lord Bryce, who might have been considered not only to know Ireland from past experience, but to speak with his hand on the mental pulse of the American people on this matter, strongly advised clemency in the following letter to the *Westminster Gazette*, in which he endorsed the advice of Sir West Ridgeway, a former Under-Secretary for Ireland:—

"Permit me to express hearty concurrence with Sir West Ridgeway in the advice which his thoughtful letter of yesterday contains. He knows, as others who have lived in Ireland or have studied her history know, that excessive severities have done far more harm by provoking afresh revengeful disaffection than punishment has ever done to quell it. This was eminently true of the rebellion of 1798, suppressed with a cruelty which shocked the humane minds of the Viceroy (Lord Cornwallis) and Sir Ralph Abercromby. The abortive rising of 1848 (which I am old enough to remember) was treated with a comparative leniency which the public opinion of that day approved, and which was justified by the result. Its chiefs did not become heroes.

"That condign punishment should be meted out to a few of those most responsible for this mad outbreak in Dublin, with its deplorable bloodshed, is inevitable. But this once done, a large and generous clemency is the course recommended by wisdom as well as by pity, and is all the more fitting because it will be a recognition of the fact that the rising was the work of a handful of persons, mostly ignorant, unbalanced visionaries, and is unequivocally condemned by the vast majority of the Irish people.—I am, faithfully yours,

"BRYCE.

"FOREST ROW, SUSSEX, *May 4th.*"

By this time, however, the matter had almost reached the character of a "pogrom." Not only had the seven signatories of the famous proclamation been executed, but every day brought another victim to the wall and told of another long list of sentences to penal servitude and other penalties, while deportations—the old Cromwellian touch, when the West Indies were peopled with Irish political offenders—reached the colossal figure of over two thousand.

Militarism is of course always a last painful resort, but there were some who seemed to look upon it as an end in itself. A writer in the *Spectator* said Lord Kitchener must be made Lord-Lieutenant, as the situation called for a soldier, and the hero of Omdurman was the nearest approach to the good old Cromwellian type.

The *Irish Times*, more English than the English themselves, then came out with the following amazing solution:—

"We hope that martial law will be maintained in Ireland for many months. When the time comes for its removal, the change to civil government ought to be smooth and gradual. This end can best be secured—in fact can only be secured—by the presence at the Viceregal Lodge of a soldier who, having taken his part in government under martial law, will be able to transmit the spirit of military administration to the civil instruments of the State."

The situation had reached a crisis, and it was then, and not till then, that the true feeling of the country came out in John Dillon's outburst that be Sir John Maxwell's character what it might—and he confessed to never having heard of him in his life—"he would refuse, and Ireland would refuse, to accept the character of any man as the sole guarantee of a nation's liberty," and the idea of military discretion fell dead at the phrase, shot through the heart.

It was high time too, for, as the case of Sheehy Skeffington proved, that discretion had been so discreet as to be unaware of its own acts, the investigation being promised after execution, which was just our whole complaint against the Germans in Belgium.[1]

The case was particularly striking, as it was only because he happened to be a well-known public man that any attention was paid to it, and it tended to give credence to the horrible rumours which now began to spread through Dublin of the secret carnage which was supposed to have taken place during what was euphemistically called "the rounding-up of the rebels" and "house-to-house visitation," while the citizens of Dublin were confined to their own houses under penalty of death if they stirred out without a permit after certain hours: and one has only to walk through the slums to hear the colossal proportions which these rumours have already attained, and which nothing but public civil investigation will stay.

I had noticed Sheehy Skeffington myself upon the Tuesday, looking very anxious and perplexed, and walking by himself without arms, and the point struck me at the time because of the remark of my companion that it was rather strange that he did not seem to be in any way officially connected with the rebels.

It was in Sackville Street—just at the time when the looting was being carried on in North Earl Street, where they had been making a barricade—and with a paper in his hand, possibly the very notice he was contemplating, he went in the direction of the Post Office porch, as if to go in and consult about something that was on his mind: again I presume to try to stop the looting, for a couple of hours later I saw the crowd of looters scattered several times by the firing of shots in their direction; and when the Imperial Hotel was raided, a Sinn Feiner told me not to be alarmed at this when leaving the city, as they were only blanks and intended to prevent the wholesale robbery that was going on.

As a matter of fact, as his wife afterwards explained, Skeffington, far from taking any part in the rising, was actually helping to look after the innocent victims of the affray, such as the Dublin Castle officer who was bleeding to death in the street, and this at imminent personal danger to himself; and at the time of his arrest near Portobello Bridge was actually engaged in the work of trying to stop the looting, having just come back from a meeting called to that effect, and had been putting up the following poster:—

"When there are no regular police in the streets it becomes the duty of the citizens to police the streets themselves, to prevent such spasmodic looting as has taken place.

"Civilians (both men and women) who are willing to co-operate to this end are asked to attend at Westmoreland Chambers (over Eden Bros.) at five o'clock on this (Tuesday) afternoon.

"FRANCIS SHEEHY SKEFFINGTON."

Far from being a combatant, he was on principle a pacifist, and thus opposed to all use of physical force; but perhaps it is better to let his own wife tell the story:—

"After he was arrested and had been sentenced to death," to use the statement which she issued to the Press, "he refused to be blindfolded, and met death with a smile on his lips, saying before he died that the authorities would find out after his death what a mistake they made."

Now, the concession of the mere possibility of such a colossal blunder was, of course, the admission of the whole of John Dillon's contention— namely, that, whatever might happen in Egypt, Ireland was right in not accepting the discretion of any man as the sole guarantee of her liberties.

For if it could happen in such an eminent case, there could hardly be any doubt but that there was considerable truth in the rumours that similar catastrophes were taking place all over Dublin, and indeed all over Ireland, and this in such a way as to madden the Irish people, and spread, if not insurrection, at least disaffection and bitterness from one end of the country to the other; but it is useless, before an official investigation, to go into such examples as the Eustace Street and King Street cases. Public investigations at the moment, however, would restore no lives, and possibly only endanger the chances of reconciliation, which is the one great need of Ireland in the name of Empire.

Quite apart from any examples, however, John Dillon maintained that the system in itself was far more likely to prejudice than to attain the very ends expected of it, "for, if they only knew it, the British Cabinet had far less power in Dublin than the Kildare Street Club and certain other institutions which were running the military authorities;" but he struck the keynote of the situation when he said: "Ours is a fighting race, and, as I told you when I was speaking before on the Military Service Bill, it is not a Military Service Bill that you want in Ireland. If you had passed a Military Service Bill for Ireland it would have taken 150,000 men and three months' hard fighting to have dealt with it. It is not a Military Service Bill that you want in Ireland; it is to find a way to the hearts of the Irish people, and when you do that you will find that you have got a supply of the best troops in the whole world."

Yet what John Dillon resented most, as indeed every moderate man in Ireland resented it, was the insinuation that the rising had been nothing more nor less than an orgy of murder by a band of criminals, so that it accordingly rendered every single Sinn Feiner liable to be shot at sight, whether he had actually taken part in the insurrection or not.

For this conception the band of English journalists who had been sent over under escort to the captured capital were much to blame. With pens reeking with the description of Hunnish crimes, they wrote their accounts of "nameless atrocities" which were supposed to have taken place in Dublin, and which, if they astounded their English readers, absolutely amazed their Irish ones.

The danger of this hate campaign which may be all very well when it is intended to rouse the somewhat lethargic Briton to fight against a race of which he knows next to nothing otherwise; but was doubly dangerous when applied to one's fellow-countrymen in the name of a party, and were it employed, say, against Wales or Scotland would soon prove disastrous, for Scotchmen and Welshmen would rise in protest to a man—which is just what Irishmen did at the "hate" wave.

Yet there was another reason—viz. the veracity and moderation of the British Press—at stake: the Press on whose veracity and moderation Irishmen depended for their motives for going away to fight for England, and this excess tended, so to speak, to tear down every recruiting poster in the country.

Now, had the British censor refused to allow any mention of the rising at all in the English Press, it might have been unjust to Ireland, but it would have been far juster to England. Much the same applies to the English

Churchmen and their Church. When the Rev. R. J. Campbell, in a Sunday illustrated, discovered that Holy Writ had already long before the rising declared in favour of Castle government and conscription for Ireland, Irish sinners felt inclined to say: "So much the worse for Holy Writ." And when the Rev. Lord William Cecil, preaching at Hatfield, summed up the ethical situation in a confusion between the meaning of pride and patriotism, Dublin wits thanked him for the phrase, and remarked that indeed it had long been so, but ne'er so well expressed, and amplified the cynical aphorism to "whenever Irishmen are patriotic it is in reality nothing but pride, yet whenever Englishmen are overproud it is nothing but the height of patriotism."

None, in fact, could have damaged the English cause in this crisis more than the English did themselves, in spite of all the Irish Nationalists were doing to help them out of the difficulty; for, as one wit remarked, the whole catastrophe had been precipitated not by English Tories so much as Irish Unionists—men, who it is difficult to say whether they misrepresent England more to Irishmen than they do Irishmen to the English, and a class which has ever got England into all Irish crises and never got her out of a single one.

For the main point about the rebellion that struck Nationalists, who, after all, were the vast majority of the Irishmen who at all mattered, was not so much the incidental crime or heroism as the utter folly of the enterprise. "Separatism" was, and will ever be probably, an economic, racial, and Imperial impossibility; yet it was just this point that was forgotten in the heat of the combat by Englishmen, with a few noble exceptions, of course.

Instead of expounding the folly of the undertaking, they preferred to dilate upon the criminality of methods and the character of the Sinn Feiners, which is just where they fell into the most fatal mistake of all and made the aftermath what it has been since—a far more complicated problem to deal with than ever existed before the rising or in the rising itself. Thus, when Sir Edward Carson raised his Volunteers in Ulster he had calculated most upon the moral effect the spilling of blood would have upon Englishmen. The Sinn Feiners had calculated upon exactly the same psychological factor with their countrymen.

When the Government had refused to take their arms by force, which Unionists were in their hearts hoping they would, the refusal left them powerless and discredited, save in the eyes of cinema operators, who only looked upon them as so much copy.

When the authorities proposed, after this example, to take the arms of the Sinn Feiners and leave the other two bodies in possession of theirs, they were, in fact, deliberately provoking rebellion; but not only this, but unconsciously they were also strengthening the cause of the Sinn Feiners, who, like the Covenanters, looked more to the moral effect than to the material results of their efforts.

Once the link of race had been appealed to, of course every attack that reflected in any way upon the character of the fighters was resented by the whole nation as a matter of honour, and that was what led John Dillon, provoked by countless insinuations and accusations to his onslaught upon the principle underlying the wholesale executions and deportations.

Had these penalties been inflicted upon those who had perpetrated the "cold-blooded murders" of the first few days, whose cry for vengeance had been voiced by Sir Arthur Conan Doyle, it would have been equally a matter of national pride to see the culprits were yielded up to justice; but "it was not these murderers that were being pursued," as Dillon pointed out; it was the rank and file of the insurgents, and these had, by almost universal admission, behaved in a manner absolutely beyond reproach as fighting men. He admitted they were wrong, but they fought a clean fight, and they fought with superb bravery and skill, and no act of savagery or act against the usual customs of war, that he knew of, had been brought home to any leader or any organized body of insurgents.

The House was inclined to resent the tribute—as much as to say that they were nothing but a pack of cowards—and this brought out a characteristically telling taunt, namely, "that it would be a damned good thing for England if her soldiers had been able to put up as good a fight as did these men in Dublin—three thousand men against twenty thousand with machine guns and artillery"—which, coming at the very moment of the announcement of the fall of Kut, must have been particularly galling.

Now, it was doubly a pity that such a controversy had been aroused, for, as most intelligent people in Dublin had begun to admit, it had been a heroic if tragically mad combat from the beginning.

Not that there had not been the most cold-blooded murders, I repeat, upon the part of some of the rank and file within the first few hours, when every representative of the law was suddenly attacked unawares, as if there had been a formal declaration of war; but from the first moment that they had felt their position nothing can be attributed to the rebel leaders which was not in the most complete accord with military precedent.

Indeed, not a few of the soldiers were struck by the self-control of the Volunteers, and the sense of discipline that pervaded their ranks; nor was it surprising, considering that while some of the Derby boys had only been in khaki for a couple of months the Volunteers had been in training ever since the beginning of the war, going through route marches, manœuvres, and sham fighting week by week and, towards the end, night by night.

True, the money may have been appropriated from such Government supplies as fell into their hands, and there is no doubt that technically they had no right to such stores; but they had every precedent, and there is even a story which tells of one of the leaders particularly asking one of the captured military to see that the safe in the G.P.O. was not touched.

There were certainly no cases of prisoners surrendering and being instantly shot; nor did civilians complain of any wanton looting of the occupied premises, though at Jacobs's and Boland's full use was made of the stores; nor were there any of the Volunteers found drunk. Certainly they should have prevented looting, but it was a duty as much incumbent upon any civilian.

In other words, in so far as it could reflect upon the national character, there was little that could be reproached against the movement save its insensate folly and, of course, the technical criminality of revolt.

On the whole the thing was on a far higher ethical plane than the methods employed by the Fenians, as well as more widespread, and the thing was far and away more dignified than poor Smith O'Brien's rising, which ended, as it began, in a humble cabbage-patch.

Some of their bullets were of course of the vilest type, inflicting ghastly wounds; but I heard of no misuse of the white flag—in fact, when the ladies who had been found in the College of Surgeons were offered their freedom as non-combatants because they had merely been doing hospital work, they refused on the ground that as they were in full sympathy with the movement they claimed the full honours of the penalties of failure.

Two things, however, must be mentioned—the one was their use of civilian clothes, and the second was their employment of "sniping" methods, both of which were highly dangerous to the rest of the non-combatant population.

With regard to the first—the use of civilian clothes—everybody who possessed a uniform wore it, but the enthusiasm of the recruits outran the means of equipment; and in any case it was adopted equally by the military, who in not a few cases owed their lives to a quick change into mufti, and who in other cases spent most of Monday and Tuesday in Sackville Street in smart lounge suits as passive spectators of the scene, when as a matter of fact they were merely spying out—and of course rightly so doing—the movements of the Sinn Feiners, together with their strength and dispositions, and then 'phoning up the information to headquarters.

Naturally it was a method of operations which greatly endangered the *bona fide* civilian, but on the whole he suffered more at the hands of the military than the Volunteer; in fact, over and over again I came across instances, sometimes of ignorance, sometimes of anger, sometimes of sheer recklessness, of the troops firing at anyone who appeared in certain localities.

As regards the general "sniping" methods employed in the whole of the Dublin rising it is hard to speak: certainly many of the Sinn Feiners would have preferred a fight in the open, and the soldiers—especially at Mount Street Bridge—felt it desperately unfair, but, under the circumstances, it became the only chance of the rebels, just as the use of shells was that of the military.

The extreme Irish loyalist merchant, of course, would have none of this; he denounced them all with the words "cowards, murderers, and criminals" in the full sense of the terms, and anyone who differed from him had Sinn Fein sympathies, and was on the list of suspects, which was rather unfair, not so much to the Sinn Feiner himself, who knew he could not have got any justice from him in any case, but unfair to the soldier and unfair to England. Thus, while elderly retired colonels and academic professors called for drastic vengeance on the scoundrels, what impressed such men as Colonel Brereton, who had actually had the experience of falling into their hands in the G.P.O., was "the international military tone adopted by the Sinn Feiners" and their peculiarly high standard of character.

"They were not," he declared, "out for massacre, for burning, or for loot. They were out for war, observing all the rules of civilized warfare, and fighting clean. So far as I saw they fought like gentlemen (?). They had possession of the restaurant in the Courts, stocked with spirits and champagne and other wines, yet there was no sign of drinking. I was informed that they were all total abstainers. They treated their prisoners with the utmost courtesy and consideration—in fact, they proved by their conduct what they were—men of education, incapable of acts of brutality, though, also, misguided and fed up with lies and false expectations."

Accordingly, upon their liberation, just before the surrender, the Colonel was profuse in his gratitude for the most unexpectedly generous treatment he himself and his fellow-prisoners had received at their hands.

Such stories came as rather awkward comments on the indiscriminate prosecutions that followed when the tables were reversed, and it was rather a relief when English Conservative papers were at last forced in the name of Empire to abandon the attitude taken up by Irish Unionist organs in the name of the Castle; for it must have been compelling evidence indeed that made the *Daily Mail*, of all newspapers, come out with the following, so to speak, unsolicited testimonial, which many an Ulster organ would have preferred to close down rather than publish:—

"The leaders were absolute blood-guilty traitors to Britain, but in some ways their sentiments were worthy of respect," said the writer. "Theirs was an intense local patriotism. They believed in Ireland. They believed that she would never prosper or be happy under British rule. They knew that there were 16,000 families in Dublin living on less than one pound a week. They saw the infinite misery of the Dublin slums, the foulest spot in Europe, where a quarter of the total population are forced to live in the indescribable squalor of one-room tenements—I quote from official records—and they believed that this was due to England's neglect (as, indeed, it was), and that the Irish Republic would end these things. Therefore they struck, and as far as they could exercise direct control over the rebel army they tried to fight a clean fight. They begged their followers not to disgrace the Republican flag. They posted guards to prevent looting. They fought with magnificent courage. Nevertheless, their control was not far-reaching, and they were disgraced by the anarchy of some of their followers. But it is necessary to point out their virtues, because it is those and their ideals that non-rebel Irishmen are remembering to-day."

FOOTNOTE:

[1] Cf. the telegram received by the Prime Minister from the man in whose discretion the whole British Legislature had placed its absolute confidence: "Mr. Skeffington was shot on morning of 26th April without the knowledge of the military authorities. The matter is now under investigation. The officer concerned has been under arrest since 6th May."

CHAPTER THE SIXTH

SINN FEIN—GERMAN GOLD

Two questions here confront us before going from the mere dramatic narrative of the rebellion to its critical consideration.

The first is, What exactly is Sinn Fein? and secondly, How far was the rising actuated by German gold?

The words "Sinn Fein" mean literally "We ourselves," *not* "Ourselves alone," and, as the title and expression of a movement, are the antithesis of what they term "Parliamentarianism," or "help from outside": but I know no better definition of it than the passage in the writer in the *Irish Year-book* article on "The Ethics of Sinn Fein."

"We are always telling the Parliamentarians that we need not wait for the Act of the British Parliament to make Ireland a Nation. We ought equally to remember that we do not require an Act of the British Parliament in order ourselves to become pure or temperate, or diligent or unselfish. Our liberty—our real liberty—the liberty both of ourselves and our country—is in our own hands. England cannot crush or kill it, or even seriously injure it. England can only remain in Ireland, indeed, as long as our character is weaker than her guns. Guns are stronger than middling character. Against real character, passionate, determined, and organized, they are less availing than children's catapults. English domination feeds and thrives on weak character. When every Nationalist makes his or her character strong and self-reliant and beautiful, English domination will die from sheer lack of sustenance. If you are weak of will or base in your character, you are as valuable a support to the English garrison in Ireland as though you hated the Irish language and imported all your clothes from Yorkshire. *The only way to be a patriotic Irishman is to do your best to become a perfect man.*"

The necessity for individual action, to continue the illustration of its spirit, is emphasized by a very wholesome phrase. It is that "the only part of the Irish Nation which a good many of us have any chance of setting free immediately is ourselves." In other words, no Parliament can make a nation free—not even a native Parliament; or, as Arthur Griffith puts it, "Every Irish man or woman's self is the Irish Nation."

With this no one of course would quarrel, but it does not follow, as the Gaelic element in Sinn Fein seemed to think, that "every Irishman who does not speak Irish is against his will a representative of English

Domination in Ireland and striking a blow at his country's heart." For when we come to consider it, English literature owes not a little to the Celtic spirit, as on the other hand Ireland of to-day contains not a little of the Saxon strain.

The attempt on the part of the Sinn Feiners therefore to establish such an extreme and antiquated definition was strictly against nature—a retrospective move, in other words, as against the blending progressive force of evolution represented by Parliamentarianism.

At the same time it would be hard to find a more fruitful, inspiring, or elevating passage than the following:—

"Choose the Ireland that you think is best, and fashion yourself in its likeness. If you wish to see Ireland become a perfect country, a kingdom of God, do you yourself become a perfect individual, a kingdom of God. The perfect country can only be established by individual men and women, who are striving after perfection—perfection not only in an imaginary Irish nation which is outside themselves, but in the actual Irish nation which is within themselves, in their own brains and hearts and sinews, to mar or to make beautiful as they will."

The Sinn Fein theory of the interdependence of the State and the individual is also worth noting:—

"I realize, of course," says the writer, "that it would be equally true, or nearly so, to say that *it is only the perfect State that could produce perfect men and women, and so my argument may appear to run in a circle. The State and the individual react on each other, however, each helping the other forward on the way towards some ultimate decency.* Some thinkers lay too much stress on the part that must be played by the State in producing the perfect individual; others have their minds occupied too exclusively by the part played by the individual in bringing about the perfect State. The man with broad views will, I think, see that both progressive individuals and a progressive State are necessary, that they are complementary one to the other. He will aspire after a free and self-reliant Ireland, and the first thing he will do in order to realize his aspirations will be to make himself self-reliant and free—free from everything that is shameful and ignoble, as he wishes to see his country free from the shame of foreign conquest and the ignominy of English rule. He will attempt to become himself among his neighbours what he wishes to see Ireland among the nations—conspicuous for honour and courage, and courtesy and virtue."

As regards the best methods of propagating Sinn Fein, the writer lays stress upon "example being better than precept," and then he remarks: "If the average professing Nationalist had been a perceptibly finer character than the average professing Unionist during the last half-century, all the noble men and women in Ireland would by the law of their natures have been attracted to the national banner."

The one blow which the Sinn Feiner strikes is at the unreality of the usual political distinctions of Nationalists and Unionists; both have their demonstrations, the writer points out, at which political speakers make speeches consciously insincere, but justified by a sort of traditional instinct; and both crowds go home equally convinced of the intolerance of their opponents, relying for victory "on the strength of their fists and lungs," but all the thinkers despise it all, and this to such an extent that he is led on to remark: "If an impartial spectator were to go to an ordinary Green demonstration in Ireland, he would probably be inclined to be an Orangeman; while if he were to attend an Orange demonstration he would probably come away feeling strangely sympathetic towards Nationalism."

Which, after all, is only what every independent writer and thinker has been bellowing forth for the past generation.

With regard to the employment of physical force there is this significant passage:—

"Whatever is to be said in favour of the use of physical force against England, there is nothing to be said in favour of Irishmen making use of it against each other. It would be as wrong, for instance, for Sinn Feiners to wreck a meeting of Parliamentarians as it would be for Parliamentarians forcibly to break up a meeting of Sinn Feiners. You might compel timid people to join you in this way, and you would win the support of that great body of people that likes always to be on the stronger side. But it is not in the hands of the timid and the selfish that the destinies of Ireland are. *The destinies of Ireland are in the hands of the free and noble men and women of Ireland whom you can persuade, but could never compel, to join you*"; and he ends up: "If you had all the force of all the Empires in the world at your back you could not increase the number of genuine Nationalists in Ireland by one"—which is perfectly true.

In policy it is both selfish and altruistic: as a national movement its aim is "Ireland first and Ireland alone and Ireland always"; as an individual movement it inculcates that "no personal sacrifice is too great for one's country," and it is probably this last feature that drew the younger generation in thousands to its standards, and no doubt will continue to do so, for in this sense of self-reliance Sinn Fein will continue to exist as long as there is a single Irishman in Ireland.

As to the constitution of "Sinn Fein," it differs very little in ideal from that of average Nationalism, save in the respect of its application, and may be quoted in full, in view of its present interest and the importance of fully appreciating at the present critical moment what Sinn Fein really is.

Sinn Fein means, as we have already seen, literally "Ourselves," and is the title and expression of a movement which denies the lawful existence of the Incorporating Union in contradistinction to Unionism (which see) and Parliamentarianism (which see). Sinn Fein declares Ireland to be by natural and constitutional right a sovereign State, and teaches that the election of Irishmen to serve in the British Parliament is treason to the Irish State, as no lawful power exists, has existed, or can exist in that Parliament to legislate for Ireland. It advocates the withdrawal of the Irish representation from Westminster, and the formation in Ireland of a voluntary legislature endowed with the moral authority of the Irish nation. The constitution and aims of the Sinn Fein organization are as follows:—

CONSTITUTION.

"The object of Sinn Fein is the re-establishment of the Independence of Ireland.

"The aim of the Sinn Fein Policy is to unite Ireland on this broad National platform.—1st. That we are a distinct nation. 2nd. That we will not make any voluntary agreement with Great Britain until Great Britain keeps her own compact which she made by the Renunciation Act of 1783, which enacted 'that the right claimed by the people of Ireland to be bound only by laws enacted by His Majesty and the Parliament of that Kingdom is hereby declared to be established, and ascertained for ever, and shall, at no time hereafter, be questioned or questionable.' 3rd. That we are determined to make use of any powers we have, or may have at any time in the future, to work for our own advancement, and for the creation of a prosperous, virile, and independent nation.

"That the people of Ireland are a free people, and that no law made without their authority or consent is, or ever can be, binding on their conscience.

"That the General Council of County Councils presents the nucleus of a National authority, and we urge upon it to extend the scope of its deliberation and action; to take within its purview every question of national interest, and to formulate lines of procedure for the nation.

"That national self-development through the recognition of the duties and rights of citizenship on the part of the individual and by the aid and support of all movements originating from within Ireland, instinct with national tradition and not looking outside Ireland for the accomplishment of their aims, is vital to Ireland."

Sinn Fein has been formed to re-establish a National Government in Ireland, and, pending its establishment, advance that object by:—

I. The introduction of a Protective System for Irish Industries and Commerce by combined action of the Irish County Councils, Urban Councils, Rural Councils, Poor Law Boards, Harbour Boards, and other bodies directly responsible to the Irish people.

II. The establishment and maintenance under the direction of the General Council of County Councils or other authority approved by the people of Ireland of an Irish Consular Service for the advancement of Irish Commerce and Irish Interests generally.

III. The re-establishment of an Irish Mercantile Marine to facilitate direct trading between Ireland and the countries of Continental Europe, America, Africa, and the Far East.

IV. The General Survey of Ireland and the development of its mineral resources, under the auspices of the General Council of County Councils or other national authorities approved by the people of Ireland.

V. The establishment of an Irish National Bank and a National Stock Exchange under charter from the General Council of County Councils.

VI. The creation of a National Civil Service embracing all the employees of the County Councils, Rural Councils, Poor Law Boards, Harbour Boards, and other bodies responsible to the Irish people, by the institution of a common national qualifying examination and a local competitive examination (the latter at the discretion of the local bodies).

VII. The establishment of National Courts of Arbitration for the speedy and satisfactory adjustment of disputes.

VIII. The establishment of a National System of Insurance of property and individuals.

IX. The control and management of transit by rail, road, and water, and the control and management of waste lands for the national benefit by a national authority approved by the people of Ireland.

X. The control and management of the Irish sea fisheries by the General Council of County Councils or other national authority approved by the people of Ireland.

XI. The reform of Education to render its basis national and industrial by the compulsory teaching of the Irish Language, Irish History, and Irish manufacturing and agricultural potentialities in the primary system, and, in addition, in the University system the institution of the degrees of Doctor of Agriculture and Doctor of National Economics.

XII. The non-consumption so far as practicable of articles paying duty to the British Exchequer.

XIII. The withdrawal of all voluntary support to the British Armed Forces.

XIV. The non-recognition of the British Parliament as invested with constitutional or moral authority to legislate for Ireland, and the Annual Assembly in Dublin of persons elected by the voters of the Irish cities and counties, and delegates from the County, County Borough, Urban and Rural Councils and Poor Law and Harbour Boards to devise and formulate measures for the benefit of the whole people of Ireland.

XV. The abolition of the Poorhouse System and the substitution in its stead of adequate outdoor relief to the aged and the infirm, and the employment of the able-bodied in the reclamation of waste lands, afforestation, and other National and reproductive works.

At what precise point the Sinn Feiners became "Republicans" it is hard to say, and it was the greatest mistake that they ever made—some will say, perhaps, their only one—but it must have been due either to the influence of Sir Roger Casement or James Connolly.

Before this amalgamation it might have been said to have corresponded in methods to the ideals of the English Fabians and Economists like Sidney Webb and H. G. Wells.

Had it proclaimed the motto "Put not your trust in soldiers" with the same vigour as it had continuously preached "Put not your trust in Parliamentarians," it would undoubtedly have become the party of the future.

It was, in fact, a protest against "oratory, oratory, oratory," and preached a doctrine of "works, works, works," but with such vehemence as to become, like everything else in Ireland, eventually political, and when "Carsonism" became a recognized principle of legislation, military from sheer necessity. It might have been said to have been the only ideal truly national, in that it endeavoured to unite, and in many cases did unite, Nationalist and Orangeman, and did this to such an extent as to threaten to drain both parties, and consequently incurred their jealousy.

Not only were the distinctions of Catholic and Protestant abolished by "Sinn Fein," but even those of Liberal and Conservative as well, and in some cases landlord and tenant, master and man.

To bring about this fusion an intellectual group arose, which was gradually, as we have said, drawing to itself some of the best brains and hearts of the nation, and these, working hand in hand with the social reformers, brought abstract theories into touch with concrete realities.

So far so good: their only enemies were the official Parliamentarians, but then, as their methods were diametrically opposed, this was only what was to be expected.

Both stood forth as rival means to an immediate end—the peace, unity, and prosperity of Ireland—and with the advent of the Liberals, which apparently was to give the Parliamentarians victory within the span of a couple of years at most, the organization became a negligible quantity.

Indeed, they voluntarily withdrew from opposition for fear it should be said that in a moment of acute difficulty they had hampered any Irishman in winning liberties for Ireland, and their daily newspaper was withdrawn.

As year after year passed, however, and Home Rule seemed to hang upon a snap division, and its hypothetical results possibly hung up for another generation, Sinn Feiners grew stronger and stronger as English opposition to the Parliamentarians grew in strength, and they once more reiterated their old principle that, Home Rule or no Home Rule, much could be done by individual effort, and that eventually, even under self-government, they would have to depend upon themselves alone, and they pointed to the Hungarian example of national regeneration outside politics.

At the first they were not, strictly speaking, in opposition at all to, but rather complementary of, the politicians; but the first moment that Carson's followers began to arm, ostensibly against them both, there arose a general cry from Nationalist Sinn Feiner and Gaelic Leaguer alike, to take measures for self-defence, which gradually grew into a volunteer organization on the lines already in force in Ulster.

From the first it must be said that John Redmond was radically opposed to any appeal to arms, even as a threat, staking all upon a Constitutional movement.

Hence in the winter of 1913-14 arose the first body of what were then called Nationalist Volunteers, the leading spirits being Mr. Eoin MacNeill, Professor of Irish in the National University, and Sir Roger Casement.

John Redmond was continually appealed to to come in with them, but as often refused, until it became a certainty that Home Rule would be placed upon the Statute Book, when he ultimately consented; but only on condition that he had the nomination of half the controlling committee—a demand which was somewhat resented.

Strange enough, it was the *Irish Times* which criticized John Redmond the most mercilessly of all for his attitude; and the passage is well worth referring to (June 6, 1914), if only as a testimony to the character both of the Irish leader and his opponents as well. The Sinn Fein leaders were then "all that was best in the country," John Redmond "all that was worst."

When the war-cloud loomed up in the horizon of Europe, the Nationalist Volunteers were indeed still one, though the opposition between the two parties was still alive, but at this point a new phase was entered into.

John Redmond, it will be remembered, upon the declaration of hostilities, at once offered the assistance of the Nationalist Volunteers to defend the shores of Ireland. Possibly the Sinn Feiners thought they smelt conscription and militarism in this, for not only did they formally expel the Redmondites, but entered upon precisely the same tactics in regard to the present war that the Parnellites adopted during the South African War. This consisted in violent pro-German sentiments, just as there had been pro-Boer sentiments a couple of decades ago. Like the Parliamentarians of 1900, they laughed at the most extreme sentiments of self-righteousness which at once came over the English Press, in which "the hereditary foe of small nationalities" was suddenly changed into "the champion of all honour, justice, and truth in the world"—which was particularly galling, if not actually ludicrous, to a race which was so obviously the negation of any such a claim—at least, so thought the Sinn Fein element.

As in those days, this spread to recruiting, and the *Hibernian* quoted one of Joe Devlin's early poetic effusions which lucidly described the miseries existent "where the Flag of England flies." *Honesty*, another of the Mosquito Press, as it came to be called, quoted John Dillon's Tralee speech of October 20, 1901, when he said: "I see there is a gentleman coming over here looking for recruits for the Irish Guards, and I hope you will put him out if he comes," which sentiments were applied to Mike O'Leary by the Sinn Feiners of the South when he turned up, and I myself saw the eyes plucked from his posters as I passed Macroom. For Sir Roger Casement's attempt to form an Irish Brigade another parallel was taken, this time from Mr. Patrick O'Brien's Dublin speech of October 1, 1899, when he said "he would not say shame to the Irishmen who belonged to British Regiments, because he had hopes that ... instead of firing on the Boers they would fire on the Englishmen. It was encouraging to think that out in the Transvaal there was a body of Irishmen ready and willing to go into the field against England."

Meanwhile, the party which once held these views as "the immutable first principles of Irish Nationalism" and was now so vigorously loyal and energetically military, appeared to the Sinn Feiners to have changed its ground, and thus to be betraying Ireland—quite forgetting that all the while it was England that had to a large extent changed its attitude.

Thus a passage in the *Irish Republic* pilloried them in a quotation from Parnell. "Parnell," it said, "speaking at Limerick on the occasion of his receiving the Freedom of that city, foretold the corruption and demoralization which a prolonged stay at Westminster would effect in the ranks of the Parliamentary Party in the following memorable words: 'I am not one of those who believe in the permanence of an Irish Party in the English Parliament. I feel convinced that sooner or later the influence which every English Government has at its command—the powerful and demoralizing influence—sooner or later will sap the best party you can return to the House of Commons.'"

As early as October 30, 1915, many Irishmen had begun to adopt the Sinn Fein attitude in this matter so strongly that Gilbert Galbraith came out with a striking leader in *Honesty*, which, referring to the famous dictum of the defeated loyalists at the Battle of the Boyne—"Change kings, and we'll fight the battle over again"—openly advocated the change, if not of leaders, at least of the methods of leadership from Redmondism to Carsonism. "In nearly every crisis of his bitter fight with Redmond," said Gilbert Galbraith, "Carson had displayed the qualities of a successful leader with strength of character and boldness of resource, and Redmond those of a weak, temporizing Stuart, and no man since Parnell had so browbeaten, insulted, and lashed with scorn the British people."

What the Sinn Feiners admired in Carson was his scrupulous honesty in declaring what he wanted, and his gloriously unscrupulous determination to see that he got it, and they called aloud that Nationalist Ireland should find someone with the Ulster spirit to lead them.

As a matter of fact it was curiously like what actually occurred, for they found those leaders in two other Ulster men, Connolly and Casement, for Germany was merely their common tool—again a leaf out of the Carsonite book.

Whence then came this link with Germany?

It is modern, very modern indeed—in fact, contemporary, certainly accidental. Sir Roger Casement had been abroad in the tropics most of his life: he hated politics; he cannot speak German, and has had to have all his negotiations done through translators and interpreters.

His sympathy with Germany was based upon the conviction that until the freedom of the seas had been established by England's naval downfall Ireland was bound to remain in intellectual, moral, and political vassalage; but that once Germany had broken the spell, Ireland could then come freely forward among the nations of the earth, free and unfettered to fulfill her destiny. He did not, as far as I can gather, want England's downfall in itself, only Ireland's freedom: and on that freedom he wished to establish the future peace of the world, bringing Saxon and Teuton together as they are to-day together in the United States through the medium of the Celt; for the Irishman can speak with far more truth of his "German cousins" than the Englishman, at least in America; and America was to count in Sir Roger Casement's dream of world-politics. If the Clan-na-Gael did indeed forward German gold to Ireland, it was with this aim, just as it was with this aim, it was said, that the Irish in America had steadily opposed the break with Germany.

Now, it was never expected that Ireland would free herself in the coming struggle, but there is a story current that he was supposed to have obtained some guarantees—of what kind I could not find out—that in the event of Germany winning Ireland would be mentioned at the peace conference in the some category as Belgium and Poland when the principle of the re-establishment of small nationalities came up for discussion, but only upon one condition, and that was "that Ireland should rise and be able to hold the Capital for a week."

One can well imagine with what avidity such plans, with their reaction upon the very delicate negotiations now going on at Washington, would be received in Germany at the present moment. But his plans—or rather I should say his dreams—appear to have been matured long before the war; dreams dreamt in the solitude of the tropics when Europe still clasped the illusion of universal peace.[2]

It was the Carson Volunteers that gave him the idea of the possibility of a physical force movement. If Orangemen could drill, why not Nationalists; if the planter could fight, why not the native; if the hands of Government could be forced by threats and arms brought in under their very eyes, why not take advantage of it; if war was inevitable sooner or later, why not prepare?—any way, it would be as noble to die for a race's emancipation as the privileges of an hereditary officialdom.

Plan for plan, and man for man, then followed the constitution of the Irish Volunteers—Carsonism turned on Carson—and Germany "used" rather than "served" in the interests of Ireland.

When John Redmond, therefore, with the doubtful facility of oratory attempted to explain away the whole rebellion with the insinuation that the whole movement was the outcome of German gold, he must for the moment have forgotten that he was talking to men who invariably looked upon him as long ago bought up with American gold, and that he was referring to his fellow-countrymen in a protest against a class he had himself times out of number denounced as subsidized by English gold—

and Sir Roger Casement's denial of such an imputation as both insolent and insulting was as true as it was dignified.

As a matter of fact the only thing German about the whole rebellion was the "Prussianism" of the Castle, which was equally responsible for the occurrence of the rising and these harsh methods of repression which eventually—paradoxically enough—made it the moral success it has since become in the hearts of Irishmen.

FOOTNOTE:

[2] Cf. "Sir Roger Casement"—a character sketch without prejudice, by L. G. Redmond-Howard. Dublin: Hodges & Figgis.

CHAPTER THE SEVENTH

MINDS AND MEN

In considering any sudden yet organized popular movement, such as a revolution, the most important things to examine are the minds and the men that directed it, for it is only by means of these forces that simmering discontents take definite shape and concrete determination.

But it often happens that the characters of the leaders themselves and even the objective remedies they propose are quite out of keeping with the solution of the real grievances they complain of.

Once given leadership, and confidence, fidelity, and sincerity follow among the rank and file as naturally as water flows from a spring—being the common factor of humanity—and this seems to have been the case in the Sinn Fein rebellion of 1916.

On the whole they had no reason to be ashamed of their leaders, though they might have questioned their wisdom. Now, wickedness in the political sense connotes the revolt against the organized authority of the State—political foolishness, the utter impossibility of realizing a practical aim. Naturally, therefore, the law was officially bound to look upon them as a species of criminal lunatics. Public men, moreover, were forced by the very theory of government to denounce them, in consequence, as enemies, and call for the sternest penalties of retribution known to the Constitution, in order that the individual's fate might become an object-lesson to the mass.

Once having granted this, however, the civilian mind is free to make the inquiry—whether from morbid, scientific, dramatic, or emotional reasons matters little—as to what manner of men these leaders were, and what manner of minds gave the revolt its psychological aspect: but in that inquiry no criterion of loyalty except that of fidelity to their own personal convictions must be allowed to enter. Probably the most serious mistake usually made by Irish politicians is that of classing successive rebellions as the acts of traitors or martyrs, according to their respective points of view, and certainly statesmen and thinkers could make no greater error in diagnosing the present one.

Rebellions are not the outcome of innate perversity of race, but purely scientific phenomena with objective causes. First, then, let us examine the men themselves who led the revolt, before we pass on to the literature that informed and inspired it.

Sir Roger Casement was not the founder of "Sinn Fein," nor was he the originator of the Labour Movement in Ireland: he found both ready-made and used them to serve his own ideals for the future of Ireland and thus can be termed a leader.

Sir Roger Casement is an Ulsterman of the old type that was the backbone of the Rebellion of '98, when the Presbyterians of the North tried to emulate those English and Irish exiles who, persecuted out of their native shores by High Church tyranny, had laid the foundations of American liberty under Washington.

That he is a man of character, and not the "bounder and scoundrel" the Press now makes him out to be, goes without saying, or otherwise he would not have received the honour of a title at the hands of a grateful country: in fact, until his entrance into the troubled waters of Irish politics he was one of the most universally respected of our civil servants.

For ten years, from 1895 to 1905, for example, he was in the wilds of Africa, for the greater portion of his sojourn as Consul in Portuguese West Africa and then later in the Congo Free State.

After this he was sent to South America, and in 1909 he was appointed Consul-General at Rio de Janeiro. So trusted was he that when the British Government wished to investigate the labour atrocities on the Indians in the rubber forests of Peru, they chose Sir Roger Casement; and when his report was printed in 1912 it caused the profoundest stir, not merely in England, but throughout the civilized world.

This was surely a man of character and above the ordinary temptations of bribery, or else he would not in 1905 have received the C.M.G. and in 1911 knighthood—moreover, he was a man who may be said to have had ample opportunity of getting outside the narrow groove of Irish politics and seeing something of the Empire.

Yet while Irish politics had been moving with tremendous rapidity during his absence—the fateful years between 1895-1905—Sir Roger Casement seems never to have got beyond the Ulster of 1798—which I need hardly remind anyone conversant with history was as rebellious to England as was Wexford under Cromwell.

This *idée fixe* began to appear at once upon his return to Ireland in the year 1913, when he found politics in a chaos of ferment, and seeing Sir Edward Carson preparing to appeal to arms and his supporters to Germany, he too "began to indulge in treason in the same spirit as Carson and the Curragh crew," as he himself described his attitude of that time.

Possibly Germany was equally willing to sell her old rifles to both parties, but the war precipitated matters.

Autumn 1914 found Sir Roger (who, as we have already seen, had founded a body of volunteers in Ireland) in Berlin, where he was not only received at the German Foreign Office, but, in answer to an inquiry regarding the Kaiser's attitude to Ireland, was assured by the Foreign Department and the Imperial Chancellor that "Germany would never invade Ireland with the object of conquering it," and that, "supposing the fortune of war should ever bring German troops to Ireland's coasts, they would land as the forces of a Government inspired by goodwill towards a land and a people for whom Germany only wishes national welfare and national freedom." That he was not acting in any way as the representative of the nation whose ambassador he was supposed to be was amply proved by his repudiation after this adventure by the Irish leaders at home and such bodies as the Council of the United Irish League in America.

Such was the dream or delusion, however, which changed one of the most respected of British Consuls into a rebel traitor to the Empire. There is no need to insinuate selfishness or vilify his character, for he must have known his effort was bound to fail and counted the cost beforehand. The great point to remember is that the Irish people were free to make their choice and use their judgment, and they decided against him, not personally, but on the merits of the case he put before them, and there was nothing to do but to pay the penalty; and it is better on the whole for Englishmen to accept Ireland's own verdict upon Sir Roger Casement than to place him in the same rank as those who really represented Ireland against England, failed, and paid the price only too willingly.

The same might apply equally well to P. H. Pearse and James Connolly, neither of whom was by nature militant nor, indeed, "Separatist," save as a protest against not so much the theory as the reality of what went by the name of "Unionism." There seems a certain tendency among the middle classes and the mediocrities of mind in Ireland to class, ever since the days of Jim Larkin, the whole Labour Movement in Ireland as a species of hooliganism, though, strange to say, no one ever appealed more successfully or was received with more genuine enthusiasm in England than the socialist leader when he was pleading the cause of the children of the Dublin slums.

When Jim Larkin went to America, his mantle fell upon his right-hand man, James Connolly, and it is impossible to understand the rebellion without understanding the man who was a far more important, and will be a far more lasting, factor in the movement than Sir Roger Casement.

Casement used the magic hope of German help, but it was Connolly who pointed to the concrete grievances that would make any rebellion welcome to the workers.

Yet there was nothing of the wild dreamer or the hysterical patriot about James Connolly, the Ulster organizer of the Transport Union, much less anything of the hooligan.

His proper place should have been within the ranks of the Parliamentary Party, like so many of the other leaders, especially the Sinn Feiners; and it is a very significant fact that, in spite of their national claims, two of the greatest economic movements Ireland has seen since Parnell should have failed to be assimilated by the politicians—but it reflects as much upon one as the other.

Probably when he wrote his last work, a pamphlet entitled "The Reconquest of Ireland," which was printed at Liberty Hall early in 1915, he had no idea that it would mean anything more than an upward economic struggle of the submerged classes.

"The Labour Movement of Ireland," he wrote, "must set itself the Reconquest of Ireland as its final aim," and by the word "reconquest" of Ireland he means "the taking possession of the entire country, all its powers of wealth, production, and its natural resources, and organizing these on a co-operative basis for the good of all."

It is significant that there is no religious or political bigotry: the movement is right outside both Carsonism and Redmondism, as indeed their new flag, with its significant colours—green, white, and orange—symbolizes; and he repeats the hope of the United Irishmen at the end of the eighteenth century, "that our animosities were buried with the bones of our ancestors and that we could unite as citizens and claim the rights of man"—the first of which is to be able to live freely, that is, with the means of life no longer the property of a class.

He had, in fact, realized "that the old lines of political demarcation no longer served to express any reality in the lives of the people." If anything, the new movement was antagonistic to them all, for in the summing-up he had observed: "In the great Dublin lock-out of 1913-14, the manner in which the Dublin employers, overwhelmingly Unionist, received the enthusiastic and unscrupulous support of the entire Home Rule Press was a foretaste of the possibilities of the new combinations with which Labour in Ireland will have to reckon."

As I read all this once again during the height of the rebellion, with the rattle of the maxims playing upon Boland's mills immediately behind me, where a couple of hundred of the men he had described were now fighting

Labour's first war under the name of an Irish Republic, at once the whole aspect of the rebellion changed.

I still wondered, however, why it was that he had left the company of Wells and Webb and Booth, who were but his English counterparts after all, and the general policy of Fabianism, when I suddenly discovered the key not only to the man but to the movement as well, in his definition of prophecy: "The only true prophets are they who carve out the future which they announce."

This, then, was the key to it all. Every dreamer should also be a man of action, every soldier a volunteer to his own idealism; and at once I understood that strange combination between the "intellectuals" and the "workers" which formed such a unique feature of the rebellion, and which the prosperous citizens of Dublin—penned up in their houses for the first time hungry, and for the first time aware of the reality of life's struggle— could only blindly mass together under the name of "criminal lunatics," like the anarchists of Sidney Street in London some years before.

Much less could the pink-faced Derby boys understand—and so I suppose thought, because the crisis had synchronized with the European war and was aimed at a state of things tolerated by English rule, it was therefore only another indication of Ireland's double dose of original sin, which always drove her to disloyalty to her benefactor.

Dr. O'Dwyer, Bishop of Limerick, one of the ablest as well as the most independent thinkers in Ireland, has been mentioned as one of the forces of the rebellion—in fact, he was generally supposed to be one of the marked men of the Fein programme of suppression, being considered more dangerous to the realm than Connolly—in a word, he was looked upon as a red-hot Sinn Feiner. Yet if his famous Lenten pastoral be examined one will find it merely the broad Christian aspect of the war—nor would the cynical diplomatist, if we could get him to be candid, say he was far wrong in his facts.

Thus, for example, speaking of the only possible result of the prolongation of the war to final victory for either party, he says:—

"No one can foresee even the smallest part of the consequences of this war. One thing, however, is certain, that it will leave the world in a condition of the direst poverty. The destruction of capital is enormous, not in one country, but in all of them. If the war ceased to-morrow it would have impoverished all Europe beyond recovery for generations, but that poverty, by itself, will probably be the least of its evils. It will mean the paralysis of industry, the restriction of commerce, unemployment on a scale that has never been known before, and it is an anxious question how a hitherto powerful, well-paid, well-organized population of workers will submit to the altered state of things. We have had, from time to time, some ugly threatenings of socialism, but we may fear that they are no more than the first mutterings of the storm which will burst upon European society as soon as this war is over.

"This terrible danger, which may be on us within the next three or four years, may well be worse than the war itself, and deluge Europe again in blood. If anyone thinks that millions of working men, trained to arms in every country in Europe, will settle down peaceably to starvation in order to help to re-amass fortunes for their 'betters,' he may have a rude awakening."

It is his attitude towards England, however, that has brought him into conflict with the recruiting authorities—yet what is the following passage, taken from his famous Lenten pastoral, but the purely Catholic attitude of a bishop who looks to the head of his Church for guidance, and seeing the Papacy neutral on the chaos, tries to keep the war fever from spreading to his own flock, for, after all, he spoke as a Churchman, not as a politician.

I think it is now universally admitted that Belgium was not the sole reason of our entrance, as it will not be the sole reason of our continuance, in the war; in a word, that it is really "British interests" that are at stake.

The learned Irish Bishop merely puts the case in so many words—had we not been engaged, the *Times* might have said, "with the impartiality of the blunt, plain-speaking Englishman."

He writes: "Then see the case of the small nationalities on whose behalf many people have believed that the war is being waged.

"What good has it done for them? What part have they played in it except that of catspaws for the larger nations that used them? Belgium delayed the German advance for two weeks and gave time to the English and French armies to rally. For her pains she has been conquered and ruined. Servia began the war by an atrocious crime, and as reparation for it might weaken Russia's aims in the Balkans, she was encouraged to resist. She, too, has played her temporary rôle and has followed in the wake of Belgium. Montenegro is the next to go; and it would seem that the great belligerent nations look to themselves only, and use their weaker neighbours for their own purposes. This war is not waged by any of the great Powers as a quixotic enterprise for lofty ideals. 'Small nationalities' and other such sentimental pretexts are good enough for platform addresses to an imaginative but uninformed people, but they do not reveal the true inwardness of this war. All the belligerents have had practical and substantial aims in view. France wants her lost provinces of Alsace and

Lorraine; Russia wants Constantinople; England wants the undisputed supremacy of the sea and riddance from German commercial rivalry; Austria wants domination in the Balkans and an outlet on the Ægean; Italy wants Trieste and what is called *Italia irredenta*; Germany wants a colonial empire and a powerful navy; and all these Powers have formed alliances and laid their plans for many a day, simply for the realization of their respective purposes.

"They planned and schemed solely for the sake of power and material gain. All the talk about righteousness is simply the cloak for ambition, and the worst of it is, that some of the belligerents have gone on repeating the profession of their disinterestedness until they have come to believe it themselves.

"Truth, and right, and justice have had very little to say to this war, which is an outbreak of materialism and irreligion. The peoples did not want this war; there is no hatred of one another amongst them: but the governing cliques in each country have led or driven them like sheep to the slaughter. God has been ignored; His law has been put aside; Christianity is not allowed to govern the relations of nations. And now the retribution is on them all. The fair dreams of victory and expanded empire and increased wealth and prosperity with which they set out have vanished long ago, and there is not a Government amongst them but is trembling for the day when it shall have to answer for its stewardship to its own people. If they knew as much in July 1914 as they do now, which of them would have plunged into war? And probably if the war goes on for another year they will curse the cowardice which kept them from manfully facing the problem of peace, for which every principle of religion and humanity, every interest, social, material, and political, of their countries, calls aloud."

All this, of course, goes to disprove that the Bishop of Limerick was a Sinn Feiner, but it also goes to prove that one cannot shake the foundations of international relations without stirring internal conditions to their very depths.

The clergy, however, were upon the whole, as they always are, with the Government, as was instanced in a hundred different cases during the rebellion.

Two of the leaders were typical of the old Fenians of darker days. One was Thomas Clarke, who earned his living by running a newsagent's and tobacconist's shop, but who was also engaged a lot in writing for many of the minor newspapers which were responsible for much of the propaganda which prepared the way for the rising.

The other—better known especially in the days of the South African War, when he was, like Colonel Lynch, one of the Nationalist heroes—was "Major" John McBride, who had actually raised an Irish Brigade to fight for the Boers against the British, and who must consequently have felt a very kindred spirit in Sir Roger Casement, who was merely repeating his tactics.

It shows how much Irish politics have progressed, however, that while all Nationalist Ireland is now watching the trial for high treason of Sir Roger Casement with indifference, the Nationalists of those days nominated McBride as Parliamentary candidate for South Mayo when a vacancy occurred by the resignation of Mr. Davitt.

He was at the time of the rising engaged as an official of the Dublin Corporation, and had been married to—and divorced from—Miss Maud Gonne, a patriot of much the same type as the Countess Markievicz.

It was he who had conducted the fight at Jacobs's factory.

McBride was really the one link between the two wars—the Anglo-Boer and the Anglo-German War, to use a Sinn Fein phrase—and if his later attitude was now impracticable, it was certainly logical and consistent with itself.

The main difference, however, was in the circumstances, and these he, like many others, refused to admit had changed.

Thus ten years before he had gone to Paris as one of the delegates from the Irish Transvaal Committee to ex-President Kruger, who told him that "he would never forget how the Irish Brigade stood by the men of the Transvaal in their hour of need."

Captain William Redmond, M.P., now in the trenches with the British Army, had also been a delegate from Ireland, and had seen Oom Paul at the Hague in much the same spirit of sympathy; but then Home Rule was not upon the Statute Book, and if that "scrap of paper" bound England, it was certainly no less binding upon Ireland, in that it had been freely entered into by her constitutional representatives.

Probably McBride thought of the motto inscribed upon the flag that the Irish Brigade had used (later presented him by one of the officials of the Boer Republic), which ran:—

"'Tis better to have fought and lost

Than never to have fought at all."

In any case his attitude remained exactly what it had been in 1909, when at the Manchester Martyr celebration he had appealed to his audience never to degrade themselves by entering the British Army, telling them that if ever they wished to fight they ought to wait for the prospect of a German invasion of Ireland.

One of the strangest figures in the rebel ranks was that of the famous Countess Markievicz—formerly a Miss Gore-Booth, daughter of Sir H. W. Gore-Booth, the head of a well-known and respected Sligo family of Cromwellian descent.

It was while in Paris as an art student some fifteen years ago that she imbibed those extreme principles of democracy—almost, one might say, anarchy—with which her name became associated on her return to Dublin after her marriage with a young Polish artist named Count Marckievicz.

Presented at Court, she was not fond of the conventional "society" circles of the Irish capital, and lived for the most part a Bohemian life of her own, becoming notorious by her extreme socialistic opinions.

During the Larkin crisis, when the transport workers and dockers went out on strike, she opened a "soup kitchen" at Liberty Hall.

She was also responsible for the organization of the "National Boy Scouts," an Irish replica of the English original, with a political bias, of course; and these soon attracted hundreds of Dublin lads, and from time to time the Countess would give them lectures and hold reviews and inspections.

These formed a considerable portion of the Citizen Army, and were probably the most violent of those elements in the Republic who disgraced the otherwise remarkable "military" combat.

One remark of the Countess's is very typical of both her temper and her temperament, and in a way prophetic.

It was supposed to have been said to a local Dundalk man, and was to the effect that if she could only shoot one British soldier she would die happy—a wish she must certainly have realized, for she was continually seen with a small rifle in her hand, and, according to a rumour, actually did shoot one on Stephen's Green.

Eoin McNeill, the able editor of the *Irish Volunteer*, is another interesting character, not only in view of the part he had taken to raise the revolutionary army, but also for the way, to use the words of John Dillon, "he broke its back" when he found out that they were to rise on that fatal Easter Monday—though this did not save him from the vengeance of the law.

In striking contrast to the rather vapid sentimentalism and abstract theorizing of many of the periodicals controlled by the Sinn Feiners was his own sheet, the *Irish Volunteer*. It was the most practical of all the periodicals, and, beyond ordinary editorials and topical articles, always contained "Orders for the Week," which included night classes and lectures and drills, while diagrams of trenches and earthworks appeared which covered the whole of Ireland.

It is only when looking back over past numbers, with their articles on night operations, local guides, reconnoitring, organization of transports, reserves, signalling, and so forth, that one sees how it is that they were able to hold up Dublin for a solid week; but Eoin McNeill owed his inspiration entirely to the men of Ulster.

Some of the men, on the other hand, were of the gentlest disposition. No one, for example, could be more the antithesis of the revolutionary in real life than P. H. Pearse, President and Commander-in-Chief of the Republican Army. Indeed, according to one account he was to have replaced Dr. Mahaffy as Provost of Trinity College, Dublin, in the event of the rising proving successful. Pearse was not even an Irishman, being the son of an English convert to Catholicism who had emigrated to Ireland, but he was an enthusiastic Gaelic scholar, and there was nothing he loved better than wandering among the peasantry of Galway and Connemara, while in his own establishment all the servants spoke Irish fluently.

Though he had at one time intended taking up journalism, and was even called to the Bar, he was both by profession and inclination an educationalist, being especially keen on the study of continental methods of education, such as those of Belgium and Germany.

He conducted a secondary boarding school for boys, where all the walls were decorated with the works of modern Irish artists, such as Jack Yeats and George W. Russell. He later, in order to give vent to his views, developed a gift for oratory, his oration at the grave of O'Donovan Rossa having stirred all Ireland. He was also the author of a charming little volume of short stories entitled "Josagan," or "Little Jesus," while his translations of Irish folk-lore and cradle songs were equally delicate.

Crowds of the victims, in fact, were men of character, talent, and eminence—numerous writers, journalists, poets, authors, professors; but all were classed in the same category of felons.

Indeed, it has been said that the blow was aimed as much at the freedom of the Press and the liberty of thought as the actual rising in arms; but as the majority of the sentiments maintained were but repetitions of the muzzled grievances of labour and thought in England, the effect will undoubtedly react through British democracy upon the heads of those who took advantage of the racial prejudice to crush out of opposition.

Thus John MacDermot, one of the signatories of the rebel proclamation, was editor of a paper called *Freedom,* and had already served a term of imprisonment for speeches which had been interpreted as prejudicial to recruiting. Edward de Valera, who commanded at Boland's mill, and who was sentenced to penal servitude for life, had been a professor in Blackrock College. W. O'Clery Curtis, who was deported, was a journalist, and Arthur Griffiths the able editor of the *Irish Year-book.*

Then came the disciples of the muses. Thomas MacDonagh seems to have been always more or less haunted with the vision of revolution, and as early as eight years ago produced a play entitled "When the Dawn is Come," though the insurrection it foretold was placed fifty years hence.

He, too, wrote poetry, like Pearse, under whom he was at school, but he was better known and his verse of a higher standard. He seems almost to have had an inkling of his future fate, and might also be said to have deliberately chosen the lost cause of his heart, for, in one of his earlier poems, entitled "The War Legacy," we find the following:

Far better War's battering breeze than the Peace that barters the Past,

Better the fear of our fathers' God than friendship false with their foe:

And better anointed Death than the Nation's damnation at last,

And the crawling of craven limbs in life and the curse of the coward below.

Among his publications are "Songs of Myself" (Hodges, Figgis & Co.), "Thomas Campion" (Hodges, Figgis & Co.), and a larger volume of "Lyrical Poems," reprinted by the *Irish Review.*

At the time of his death he was Lecturer in English Literature at the National University.

Probably one of the most pathetic figures of the whole revolt was that of young Joseph Plunkett, the son of Count Plunkett, whose marriage upon the morn of his execution sent such a thrill of romance through the English-speaking world when it became announced.

He too was a poet, and at one time the editor of the *Irish Review,* now no more, and he was also a contributor to the *Academy* and the *Dublin Review.*

A little volume entitled "The Circle and the Sword," published by Maunsel, is dedicated to his fellow-rebel, Thomas MacDonagh.

One poem among them is especially significant and is entitled "1867," but one feels inclined to call it 1916, for it might have been written yesterday, as he blindfold faced the levelled rifles:—

All our best ye have branded

When the people were choosing them.

When 'twas death they demanded,

Ye laughed! ye were losing them.

But the blood that ye spilt in the night

Crieth loudly to God,

And their name hath the strength and the might

Of a sword for the sod.

* * * * *

In the days of our doom and our dread

Ye were cruel and callous.

Grim Death with our fighters ye fed

Through the jaws of your gallows.

But a blasting and blight was the fee

For which ye had bartered them.

And we smite with the sword that from ye

We had gained when ye martyred them!

It is probably by the romance of his last hours, however, that he will be most remembered.

"Late on Wednesday night," as Mr. Stoker, the Grafton Street jeweller already mentioned, told me the story, "just as I was about to go home, suddenly a taxi stopped at the shop door, and a beautiful young woman stepped out and asked me to show her some wedding-rings—'the best,' as she put it, 'that money could buy.'

"She had a thick veil, but I could see that her eyes were red with weeping, and, noticing continued convulsive sobs as she spoke, I ventured to ask her the reason.

"It was then that she revealed the terrible tragedy she was about to suffer.

"'I am poor Joe Plunkett's—the rebel's—fiancée,' she said, 'and we are to be married in prison to-morrow morning, an hour before his execution.'

"I tell you it was the most pathetic thing I had ever heard in my life," continued the jeweller; "and I felt inclined to break down myself when she added: 'Oh! I can't tell you how I love him and how he loves me; we belong to each other, and even if we are only to be together for a single hour I mean to marry him in spite of everybody, in order to bear his name through life.'"

The young woman at once stepped into the same category as Sarah Curran, poor Robert Emmet's sweetheart, in the heart of everyone in Dublin as the story went round like lightning, but no one knew who she was until the next day, when we heard that she was Grace Gifford, the beautiful and gifted young art student whose portrait by William Orpen, entitled "Young Ireland," had won the admiration of all London a few years before.

Not all the character and talent and romance of these leaders, however, would have been sufficient to launch Ireland into open rebellion had there not been some concrete grievance as well which gave their words objective worth.

Style alone makes no martyrs, and the best way to understand the influence these men had upon their followers is to study the concrete grievances which they preached in season and out of season, making revolution not only sound plausible but actually practicable; and for this we must turn to the literature, which explains the remoter home causes of the rebellion.

CHAPTER THE EIGHTH

REMOTER CAUSES OF THE REBELLION

Those who think they can explain away the Sinn Fein rising of 1916 by the factor of German gold make much the same mistake as those who were so anxious to explain away the Home Rule movement by American dollars. The fact of the matter is, great movements and national uprisings should not be explained away: they should be, on the contrary, amplified, emphasized, and deeply studied.

I remember on one occasion the late W. T. Stead, when he was helping me with the biography of my uncle, Mr. John Redmond, emphasizing upon me the tremendous importance of the study of Irish problems to an Empire like ours, where nearly every one of its component nations is a repetition of Ireland.

"We have made every mistake we could possibly make as a ruling race in our government of you Irish," he said to me, "and we cannot, as we love and wish to keep our Empire, continue to perpetuate them.

"We can keep Ireland down if we like by force of arms, but we shall never be able to keep our Empire by the same means, and that is why it is so important that with such an object-lesson at our very doors we should be ever prepared to study how conquered or incorporated nations look upon our rule.

"That rule may be a protection, and it should be, but our stupidity can make it a yoke; yet of this we can be certain, that what fails to win friendship and respect in Ireland will fail to win security for our Empire when we employ those methods on nations who have it in their power to say us nay."

In other words, as long as the suppression has only been a military suppression it has been no suppression at all; any more than a delirious patient who is drugged or held down by force by a couple of hospital porters is cured by that expedient.

Moreover, all such expedients are necessarily merely temporary, and what we want to get at are the root causes of the complaint.

We must therefore fully diagnose those grievances of which the rebellion was only the outward symptom, and against which the Republic was more, after all, a symbolic protest than anything else; it was no more really intended to establish a Celtic Commonwealth than Sir Edward Carson's army was to change a Province into a Kingdom. Both were *façons de parler*, and the word "provisional" saved them from ridicule they would otherwise have deserved.

I remember speaking to a prominent Sinn Feiner only a couple of days before the revolt with a view to writing an article on the Volunteers, and this is what he said:—

"It would be very difficult for anyone to write anything just at present, for things are trembling in the balance. There is a most tremendous battle going on at the present moment at the Castle, we understand, between General Friend and Augustine Birrell—in other words, between the military and the civil authorities—and everything depends upon that issue.

"They want to take away our arms, for example, and not those of Redmond or Carson, and the latter will stand by and see it done without a word; but we know that's only the thin end of the wedge of the complete subjugation of Ireland to the soldier, as in the days of Cromwell, and even if we stand alone we will stop that.

"They don't half of them know a tenth of our power; even people in Ireland don't realize it. We are completely organized and perfectly equipped, far better even than the Ulster Volunteers are, and they will find out their mistake when they try.

"They've made two attempts already, in a hole-and-corner sort of way, at the Gaelic Press and at Liberty Hall, and the police found themselves looking into the barrels of revolvers each time. Well, all I can say is, when the day comes and they determine to strike—and we'll get wind of it—you may depend upon it the whole world will get a surprise; it will be like nothing else in Irish history for seven hundred years.

"We have our supplies at regular intervals, and our local commanders, with each province fully organized under them, and a complete system of code messages which never go through the post, but are distributed by means of secret dispatch-riders, and if the signal went forth to-night, to-morrow morning the whole of Ireland would be up in arms."

All of which, I need hardly say, I took—as everyone in my place would have taken it—*cum grano salis*, but it all came back to me the moment I heard the first shot. Especially did it flash across my mind when, bringing back to Dun's Hospital a dead Sinn Feiner, the famous document fell out of his pocket, which is strikingly similar in thought to my friend's prognostications.

According to Alderman Kelly, speaking on the Thursday before the outbreak in the Dublin Corporation, some such order had been "recently addressed to and was on the files of Dublin Castle," according to which the arrest of all the leaders of the Irish Volunteers, together with the members of the Sinn Fein Council, the Executive Committee of the National (Redmondite) Volunteers, and the Executive Committee of the Gaelic League, had been sanctioned.

Probably, however, the best diagnosis of the situation immediately preceding the outbreak was the letter published by the *New Statesman* of May 6th, that had been written as early as April 7th, and which, coming from the most eminent victim of the danger so clearly foreseen by him, must have special force at the present moment.

It was from no less than F. Sheehy Skeffington.

"SIR,—The situation in Ireland is extremely grave. Thanks to the silence of the daily Press, the military authorities are pursuing their Prussian plans in Ireland unobserved by the British public; and, when the explosion which they have provoked occurs, they will endeavour to delude the British public as to where the responsibility lies. I write in the hope that, despite war-fever, there may be enough sanity and common sense left to restrain the militarists while there is yet time.

"I will not take up your space by recounting the events that have led up to the present situation—the two years' immunity accorded to Sir Edward Carson's Volunteers in their defiant illegalities, the systematic persecution of the Irish Volunteers *from the moment of their formation (nine months before the war)*, the militarist provocations, raids on printing offices, arbitrary deportations, and savage sentences which have punctuated Mr. Redmond's recruiting appeals for the past eighteen months. As a result of this recent series of events, Irish Nationalist and Labour opinion is now in a state of extreme exasperation. Recruiting for the British Army is dead; recruiting for the Irish Volunteers has, for the moment, almost reached the mark of one thousand per week—which is Lord Wimborne's demand for the British Army. A special stimulus has been given to the Irish Volunteer movement by the arrest and threatened forcible deportation (at the moment of writing it is still uncertain whether the threat will be carried out) of two of its most active organizers.

"There are two distinct danger-points in the position. In the first place, the Irish Volunteers are prepared, if any attempt is made forcibly to disarm them, to resist, and to defend their rifles with their lives. In the second place, the Irish Citizen Army (the Labour Volunteers) are prepared to offer similar resistance, not only to disarmament, but to any attack upon the

Press which turns out the *Workers' Republic*—successor to the suppressed *Irish Worker*—which is printed in Liberty Hall.

"There is no bluff in either case. That was shown (1) in Tullamore on March 20th, when an attempt at disarming the small local corps of Irish Volunteers was met with revolver shots and a policeman was wounded—fortunately not seriously; (2) in Dublin, on March 24th and following days, when, at the rumour of an intended raid on the *Workers' Republic*, the Irish Citizen Army stood guard night and day in Liberty Hall—many of them having thrown up their jobs to answer promptly the mobilization order—armed and prepared to sell their lives dearly. The British military authorities in Ireland know perfectly well that the members of both these organizations are earnest, determined men. If, knowing this, General Friend and his subordinate militarists proceed either to disarm the Volunteers or to raid the Labour Press, it can only be because they *want* bloodshed—because they want to provoke another '98, and to get an excuse for a machine-gun massacre.

"Irish pacifists who have watched the situation closely are convinced that this is precisely what the militarists do want. The younger English officers in Dublin make no secret of their eagerness 'to have a whack at the Sinn Feiners'; they would much rather fight them than the Germans.[3] They are spurred on by the Carson-Northcliffe conscriptionist gang in London. On April 5th the *Morning Post* vehemently demanded the suppression of the *Workers' Republic*; on April 6th a question was put down in the House of Commons urging Mr. Birrell to disarm the Irish Volunteers. These gentry know well the precise points where a pogrom can most easily be started.

"Twice already General Friend has been on the point of setting Ireland in a blaze—once last November, when he had a warrant made out for the arrest of Bishop O'Dwyer, of Limerick; once on March 25th, when he had a detachment of soldiers with machine guns in readiness to raid Liberty Hall. In both cases Mr. Birrell intervened in the nick of time, and decisively vetoed the militarist plans. But some day Mr. Birrell may be overborne or may intervene too late. Then, once bloodshed is started in Ireland, who can say where or how it will end?

"In the midst of world-wide carnage, bloodshed in our little island may seem a trivial thing. The wiping out of all the Irish Nationalist and Labour Volunteers would hardly involve as much slaughter as the single battle of Loos. Doubtless that is the military calculation—that their crime may be overlooked in a world of criminals. Accordingly, the nearer peace comes, the more eager will they be to force a conflict before their chance vanishes. Is there in Great Britain enough real sympathy with Small Nationalities, enough real hatred of militarism, to frustrate this Pogrom Plot of British Militarist Junkerdom?

"Yours, etc.,

"F. SHEEHY SKEFFINGTON."

Personally, I think I can diagnose the rebellion into ten perfectly distinct factors, but by far the least of them all is Germany. Germany was the personal note which Sir Roger Casement brought in, and which left it with his failure. It was accidental and extraneous both to the Sinn Fein Volunteers and the Citizen Army, though both were willing to make use of it.

Anyone who has taken the trouble to peruse the literature which fed the movement will recognize these diverse elements under various forms which appear in different places, but they are perfectly distinct.

The most immediate cause was the undoubted intention of the authorities to disarm them—a threat which had been overhanging them for some time, and which, in view of the well-known leniency of the Government with regard both to Sir Edward Carson and John Redmond in the same matter, struck them as particularly unjust, the more so perhaps because both Sinn Feiners and Larkinites thought that the Nationalists and the Orangemen would be only too glad to combine with the Government against them if need be.

Thus, if we take the issue of the *Workers' Republic* of April 22, 1916, we find an account, quoted from the *Liverpool Courier*, of how Connolly, the Commandant of the Citizens' Army, stopped the police raid, in search of papers, on the shop of the Workers' Co-operative Society at 31, Eden Quay, having been informed of their intention.

"Connolly," says the account, "arrived on the scene just as one of the police got in behind the counter. Inquiring if the police had any search warrant, they answered that they had not. On hearing this, Mr. Connolly, turning to the policeman behind the counter as he had lifted up a bundle of papers, covered him with an automatic pistol, and quietly said: 'Then drop those papers, or I'll drop you.' He dropped the papers. Then he was ordered out from behind the counter, and he cleared. His fellow-burglar tried to be insolent, and was quickly told that as they had no search warrant they were doing an illegal act, and the first one who ventured to touch a paper would be shot like a dog. After some parley, they slunk away, vowing vengeance."

The story runs on for a column or more, and ends with further discomfiture for the police. Then one reads:—

"In an hour from the first issue of the summons Liberty Hall was garrisoned by a hundred and fifty determined armed men, and more were trooping in every few minutes. It was splendid to see the enthusiasm of the men, and when in the course of the evening all the Women's Ambulance Corps trooped in, closely followed by the Boy Scouts, excitement and longing for battle was running high in all our veins. The Irish Volunteers were also on the alert, and stood, we are informed, until after 2 a.m. on Saturday morning. Since then the hall has been guarded day and night."

The paper then goes on to speak of how "the heroic fighting at Suvla Bay, and even the valorous defence of Verdun, fades into insignificance side by side in Dublin by the Citizen Army, and describes how Liberty Hall is being guarded by day and by night," and then goes on to point out the danger which such open disregard of authority may lead to eventually.

Then follow two significant quotations, one from the *Irish Volunteer* and the other from *The Spark*. The latter is an open boast of the efficacy of arms, and runs:—

"A few thousand Irishmen, who took the precaution or providing themselves with lethal weapons of one kind or another, have, without contesting a constituency and without sending a man to Westminster, compelled the Westminster Parliament to admit publicly that it dared not pass any legislation which they, the armed men, did not choose to permit."

Eoin MacNeill's threat is hardly less significant:—

"If our arms are demanded from us, we shall refuse to surrender them. If force is used to take them from us, we shall make the most effective resistance in our power. Let there be no mistake or misunderstanding on that point.... We shall defend our arms with our lives."

Now, whatever may be thought of such sentiments, there can be no doubt whence they originated, for they are sheer Carsonism through and through; and it was, as I have repeatedly pointed out, a pure stroke of luck that it was not Belfast's City Hall instead of Dublin's Post Office that was burnt to the ground.

This physical force element, therefore, the Sinn Feiners and Larkinites had in common with the Redmondites and Ulstermen: the fact that they actually were the first to put the principle into operation is no difference at all.

In other words, we have to go deeper for a specific distinction, and that distinction is to be found in the very nature of the parties themselves who combined to form the provisional Republic.

They were two movements which had grown up outside the two Parliamentary parties and which refused to believe in Parliamentarianism as much for the simple reason that their respective watchwords had become more or less worn-out tags, out of touch with the realities of modern Irish problems, as because their leaders had, unable to assimilate them, taken up an attitude of almost personal antipathy to them and their ideals.

It is certainly a most remarkable thing how John Redmond has lost the old Parnellite grip upon the younger life of the country, and it seems hardly credible that such an attitude should be due entirely to the perversity of youth and in no way to the natural consequence of tradition-loving age; but in any case the broad fact remains, and a tone of persistent criticism seems to have taken the place of the meek obedience of other days; and newspapers, dramas, novels, criticism, and movements on all sides bear witness to it. The same, too, applies to Sir Edward Carson, whose party has to recruit in England, witness Sir F. E. Smith.

According to Mr. T. M. Healy, the whole movement was due almost entirely to the "bankruptcy of Redmondism." No doubt the justice of the accusation may be questioned, though I hold no brief for any relative, but there can be no doubt that it was the Sinn Fein attitude, and we want to see the Sinn Feiners as they saw themselves and as they saw Redmond.

The Government trusted to Redmond almost entirely, but, as Mr. Healy continues, they forgot that—

"New crystallizations were taking place. The jobbery of the official party disgusted all earnest and unselfish minds amongst the youth of Ireland. The forces of Larkinism were embittered; and the acceptance of salaries by Irish members, after their formal declaration that they would not accept them, sank deeply into the hearts of extremists.

"The Insurance Act, the killing of land purchase, and the founding of the A.O.H., sapped the foundations of belief, and it became known that 'a high official achieved his ambitions on the judicial bench only by becoming a professing Catholic and accepting initiation under the rites of Mr. Devlin's brotherhood. The staff of the *Freeman's Journal*, the official patriot organ, got endless jobs. At the same time Mr. Redmond excluded from his party, without trial or grounds, a dozen leading members opposed to this policy.'

"All that was sober, unselfish, self-respecting, and self-reliant quitted his ranks and joined the Sinn Fein movement without thought of rebellion or pro-Germanism.

"The courage of the Sinn Feiners atoned for much of their folly in the mind of those who realized that their spirit was not pro-German, but, in the main, a revolt against the conversion of Dublin Castle into a Redmondite

Tammany Hall. Their uprising was the answer to the corruption, jobbery, and judge-mongering of the Molly Maguires masquerading in the vestments of religion. Hence the wholesale arrests of men not in rebellion have evoked no protest from Mr. Redmond, 'who watches calmly the dispersal of his critics,' hoping to find a new lease of life under a new jobbing nominee."

The Larkinists were, if anything, still more out of sympathy with the official party because, in the words of Connolly, they looked upon them as no better than the English conqueror, since they took the side of the social conqueror in the economic struggles of life in the city.

This seems certainly to have a touch of truth, for if ever any body of men resembled the unfortunate victims of rural landlords it was these wretched victims of the tenement slums, the denunciation of which seemed to have no part in the official Parliamentary programme, so much so as to compel Labour to create its own party and evolve its own leader, which it had accordingly done in the person of Jim Larkin.

Now, if anyone wishes to judge James Connolly they should not look at the soldier for a week; they must examine the life-long student of economics and read his "History of Labour in Irish History" and his "Reconquest of Ireland," for it is here we have the revolution in its cause, which was just as much economic as political.

It is the custom to speak of the Larkinites with scant respect, as if they were the mad, blind multitude of the "have nots" in perpetual prey upon the "haves"; but it is quite a false idea, for they have in their movement some of those who count socially and intellectually.

Thus, for example, the training of the Citizens' Army was almost entirely carried out by Captain J. R. White, D.S.O., son of the late Field-Marshal Sir George White, whose "Labour" ideas got him three months' imprisonment only a few weeks ago.

As to the attitude of the average Dublin merchant towards the new labour party that is arising, I know of no finer apology for Larkin than the brilliant letter of "Æ." to the *Irish Times* in the days of the great strike, when he addressed the "masters of the city."

In it he warned them—the aristocracy of industry—because like all aristocracies they tended to grow blind in long authority, and to be unaware that they and their class and their every action were being considered and judged day by day by those who had the power to shake or overturn the whole social order, and whose restlessness in poverty was making our industrial civilization stir like a quaking bog. He reminded them that their assumption that they were answerable to themselves alone for their actions in the industries they controlled was becoming less and less tolerable, in a world so crowded with necessitous life; but what he chiefly held them responsible for was their incompetence as commercial men, because, with the cheapest market in the world at their command, they could never invite the confidence of investors.

What was even worse than their business incompetence, however, was, according to "Æ.," their bad citizenship, for had they not allowed the poor to be herded together so that one could only think of certain places in Dublin as of a pestilence?

"There are twenty thousand rooms in Dublin," continued the terrible indictment, "in each of which live entire families and sometimes more, where no functions of the body can be concealed, and delicacy and modesty are creatures that are stifled ere they are born." In fact, "nothing that had ever been done against them cried so much to heaven for vengeance as their own actions, such as the terrible lock-out, which threw nearly a third of the whole city on to the verge of starvation"; and he concluded:—

"You are sounding the death-knell of autocracy in industry. There was autocracy in political life, and it was superseded by democracy. So surely will democratic power wrest from you the control of industry. The fate of the aristocracy of industry will be as the fate of the aristocracy of land, if you do not show that you have some humanity still among you."

It was from such roots that the spirit of the Citizens' Army drew its inspiration (and possibly not a few of the looters as well), and it is impossible to understand the rage of these men without fully comprehending the condition in which they were compelled to live and move.

True, the revolt was not with any concrete economic end in view; but, none the less, it was coloured throughout with economic grievances.

It was the very torture of the ordinary conditions of peace that made them resent the fear of any additional burdens and sacrifices such as were demanded of their patriotism.

Yet what did patriotism and Empire mean to them, save only the doubling of their burdens and their masters' profits?

If the Scotch workman in London and the Scotch worker on the Clyde and the Welsh miner in the coalfields round Cardiff felt it, much more must the Irish docker; and it must never be forgotten that there is a triple link of blood, interest, and common sympathy between the workers of the two islands; and one has only to glance at the way the respective labour Presses of the two countries kept in touch with each other for the past year to realize how much an English labour problem the Irish political problem really was.

This brings me to some further factors which can be discerned in the rising—firstly, the fear of conscription; secondly, the hatred of militarism; and, thirdly, the chronic loathing of Castle government.

With regard to conscription, there has always been a dread of it. They had seen it come in England, and had watched anxiously the way it had been introduced and applied, and the farce of the Tribunals, whose action, in the words of the *Freeman's Journal*, would have been sufficient to cause a revolution had they behaved in Ireland as they behaved in England.

All during the summer months they had seen the cloud gathering, and Irishmen caught by a legal technicality and forced into the system; but all this came to a climax when the cry of cowardice was raised at Liverpool, as five hundred young emigrants, who would never have been helped to live for Ireland in their own country, were suddenly held up by order of the Cunard Company—which, as a matter of fact, owed nearly its whole prosperity to its coffin boats of the Famine days, and whose glaringly seductive posters had emptied Ireland, neither for America nor Ireland's sake, but purely to get the passage-money of the emigrants who were now asked to go instead and "help England to give Constantinople to Russia, even if it cost them their lives."

For they had a way of blunt speaking, these men whose everyday life was an heroic fight for the home against "Hun" poverty.

When the cry of "cowardice" was raised, however, it was high time to protest, and none voiced that protest so well as Dr. O'Dwyer, the Bishop of Limerick, who wrote the following letter to the *Munster News*:—

"SIR,—The treatment which the poor Irish emigrant lads have received at Liverpool is enough to make any Irishman's blood boil with anger and indignation. What wrong have they done to deserve insults and outrage at the hands of a brutal English mob? They do not want to be forced into the English Army, and sent to fight English battles in some part of the world. Is not that within their right? They are supposed to be free men, but they are made to feel that they are prisoners, who may be compelled to lay down their lives for a cause that is not worth 'three rows of pins' to them.

"It is very probable that these poor Connaught peasants know little or nothing of the meaning of the war. Their blood is not stirred by the memories of Kossovo, and they have no burning desire to die for Serbia. They would much prefer to be allowed to till their own potato gardens in peace in Connemara. Small nationalities, and the wrongs of Belgium and

Rheims Cathedral, and all the other cosmopolitan considerations that rouse the enthusiasm of the Irish Party, but do not get enough of recruits in England, are far too high-flying for uneducated peasants, and it seems a cruel wrong to attack them because they cannot rise to the level of the disinterested Imperialism of Mr. T. P. O'Connor and the rest of the New Brigade.

"But in all the shame and humiliation of this disgraceful episode, what angers one most is that there is no one, not even one of their own countrymen, to stand up and defend them. Their crime is that they are not ready to die for England. Why should they? What have they or their forbears ever got from England that they should die for her? Mr. Redmond will say a Home Rule Act on the Statute Book. But any intelligent Irishman will say a simulacrum of Home Rule, with an express notice that it is never to come into operation.

"This war may be just or unjust, but any fair-minded man will admit that it is England's war, not Ireland's. When it is over, if England wins, she will hold a dominant power in this world, and her manufactures and her commerce will increase by leaps and bounds. Win or lose, Ireland will go on, in our old round of misgovernment, intensified by a grinding poverty which will make life intolerable. Yet the poor fellows who do not see the advantage of dying for such a Cause are to be insulted as 'shirkers' and 'cowards,' and the men whom they have raised to power and influence have not one word to say on their behalf.

"If there is to be conscription, let it be enforced all round, but it seems to be the very intensity of injustice to leave English shirkers by the million to go free, and coerce the small remnant of the Irish race into a war which they do not understand, and which, whether it is right or wrong, has but a secondary and indirect interest for them.

"I am, dear sir,

"Your obedient servant,

" ✠ EDWARD THOMAS,

"Bishop of Limerick.

"November 10, 1915."

The seditious Press took up the cry: "Conscription had not even been applied to her own sons, yet England was applying it to Irishmen," said Gilbert Galbraith in *Honesty*; adding: "for all she wants of Irishmen is their lives that she might live," and he warned Irishmen that "she (England) who took everything they had and stripped them naked and left them like Christ to the ribald jest and sneer of the rabble in the world's back-streets, would, like every bully, try to have revenge when she got them by themselves."

Had this been mere verbal sword-play, however, I should not quote it; it was more: it was the taking up of the challenge of cowardice.

"Will you in God's name get ready to answer her?" concluded the famous article in which he appealed to these would-be exiles repatriated by force; "because, if you want to, all you have to do is to get into touch with the nearest corps of Irish Volunteers." They would give them instructions, he added pointedly, how to act, and what they did they had better do quickly, for it might be too late on the morrow.

Could one be surprised, I ask, if some of these would-be emigrants answered the taunt gun in hand?—especially when men like Captain White, who was afterwards to try to rouse the South Wales miners to endeavour to save Connolly, was telling them plainly:—

"You are fast being led into industrial slavery. You know it, and I am apprehensive and angry, but too bewildered to move. To rob you of your right over your own poor bodies is the workers' tyrant. To rob you of your sovereign power over your own will is the workers' devil.

"Awake, brothers, before your liberty is dead. Arm yourselves against your real enemies. Say to the tyrants and their agents, 'The first man who lays hands on me against my will dies.'"

All this, I say, jumps to the eyes of anyone perusing the literature that produced the rising.

It is beside the point whether such argumentation be true or false, patriotic or seditious. The only point, as far as we are concerned in this quasi-medical diagnosis of diseased mentality, is whether or not these thoughts were present in the psychology of the combatants, and I maintain that the evidence is undeniable.

The attitude of "conscientious objectors" to militarism in England is England's own affair. Yet I cannot, in my own mind, separate the personality of Sir John Simon from that of John Hampden. No doubt ship-money was necessary, and it was the patriotic thing to give it up, and no doubt the same applies to men for the Army: but when it came to the principle of the King taking money without the consent of Parliament, John Hampden thought it his duty to the traditions of his country to resist, just as Sir John Simon thought it his duty to the traditions of the British conscience to passively protest—but that again, I say, is a matter for Englishmen.

The attitude of the Irish conscientious objector, however, has always been of a more militant form, and this began to assert itself among the labour leaders in Ireland through the medium of the more outspoken of the English labour leaders. Whereas in England the masses of workers are naturally loyal, in Ireland loyalty is a sustained effort against the grain of tradition. Hence, while in England the right to rebel fell on unsympathetic soil, in Ireland it merely relit the smouldering embers of past grievances into flame.

For there had been a growing epidemic of the phrase "Shoot them," applied almost indiscriminately, like a quack panacea, by political orators to every opponent on every conceivable subject since the war, and this was producing the most evil results.

Two quotations may suffice from the work by J. Bruce Glasier on "Militarism," which was freely circulated in Dublin by means of Liberty Hall, to illustrate the strength of the feeling on this subject:—

"Although Great Britain is suffering neither from invasion from without nor insurrection from within, the military authorities are not only in command of the defences of our shores but of the civil authorities, and the whole population of the realm. The birthrights of British citizenship embodied in the Magna Charta, Habeas Corpus, and Bill of Rights are no longer inviolable. Martial Law—that is to say, military despotism—may be put in operation at will by the military commanders. Civilians may be seized and tried by Army officers, and even sentenced to any penalty short of death without appeal to trial by jury. Our War Lord is made virtual dictator. A military censorship has been established over the Press and public meetings. Military officers may enter our houses, quarter troops upon us, take possession of our horses, motor-cars, cows, pigs, and pigeons. They may commandeer schools, factories, warehouses, farms, or any other kinds of public or private property. Strikes may be declared acts of treason, Trade Union officials arrested and tried by courts martial, and soldiers used as blacklegs—and no knowledge whatever of these happenings, not even of the existence of strikes or trade disputes, may reach the general public at all if the authorities so determine...."

A phrase that seems to have done great harm, and was specially singled out by the men of Liberty Hall, was "Shoot him!"—as a form of argument employed by every Tom, Dick, and Harry orator, on every conceivable subject without the slightest constitutional authority; but it must be said it was one used by all parties.

During the Home Rule controversy, for example, the Nationalists were just as fond of employing the phrase towards Carson as during the Welsh coal strikes Conservatives were of using it towards the miners.

The danger of such doctrines in Ireland is this, that whereas in England it is the upper class principally that is militarist, in Ireland it is principally the lower class, and whereas it is the Castle authorities who are always preaching the iniquity of physical force, it is the lower classes who mainly admire it.

Realizing this, as any student of Irish history would, there should not have been the slightest doubt about the danger of employing force to men who not only had the principle of active resistance but the arms necessary to make it effective, and it has always appeared to me as the most marvellous thing the Liberals ever did that they were able to allow Ulster the full possession of arms without once provoking an occasion on which to actually put them to use.

The result of this fatal misuse of the words "Shoot him!" as a form of argument—which unauthoritative should be made a penal offence—was that the workers really feared that such irresponsible individuals if given the power would really carry out the threat, and determined to anticipate the danger by a protest in arms.

Another contributory cause was undoubtedly Castle rule, and the fear that with the holding up of Home Rule it might continue for ever, unless some effective protest were made.

The Chief Secretary was himself the foremost in admitting this to be one of the contributory causes of the rebellion.

"There are a number of contributory causes, which lately have created antipathy to constitutional methods and tended to increase in numbers. First—growing doubts about the actual advent of Home Rule. If the Home Rule Bill had not been placed on the Statute Book there must have been in Ireland and the United States a great and dangerous explosion of rage and disappointment, which when the war broke out would have assumed the most alarming proportions in Ireland. All (outside parts of Ulster) would have joined hands, whilst our reports from Washington tell us what the effect in America would have been. Still, even with Home Rule on the Statute Book, the chance of its ever becoming a fact was so uncertain, the outstanding difficulty about Ulster was so obvious, and the details of the measure itself were so unattractive and difficult to transmute into telling platform phrases, that Home Rule as an emotional flag fell out of daily use in current Irish life. People left off talking about it or waving it in the air.

"Second, in Ireland, whenever Constitutional and Parliamentary procedure cease to be of absorbing influence, other men, other methods, other thoughts, before somewhat harshly snubbed, come rapidly to the surface, and secure attention, sympathy, and support. The sneers of the O'Brienites, the daily naggings in the Dublin *Irish Independent*, also contributed to the partial eclipse of Home Rule, and this eclipse foretold danger."

Another point is worth noting in this connection, and that was the growing power, first of the Coalition and then of the Unionist clique who were capturing it. Thus says Mr. Birrell:—

"The Coalition Government, with Sir Edward Carson in it—it is impossible to describe or overestimate the effect of this in Ireland. The fact that Mr. Redmond could, had he chosen to do so, have sat in the same Cabinet with Sir Edward Carson had no mollifying influence. If Mr. Redmond had consented, he would, on the instant, have ceased to be an Irish leader. This step seemed to make an end of Home Rule, and strengthened the Sinn Feiners enormously all over the country."

A general desire for peace and a sort of Socialistic feeling of brotherhood, I should say, were two further contributory causes.

"The prolongation of the war and its dubious end," as Mr. Birrell observed, "turned many heads. Criticism was not of the optimistic type prevalent in Britain, and consequently, when every event had been thoroughly weighed, there was always a chance of Germany lending a hand."

As to the general attitude of Sinn Fein and Larkinite Ireland, it might be described as one of benevolent neutrality where, as in many cases, it was not one of actual hostility.

True, recruiting figures had reached a total quite unprecedented in Irish history (150,000), and loyalty had received an official stimulus when the Irish leader and the Lord-Lieutenant toured the provinces together; but this was discounted in the country districts by the deliberate plans of the Sinn Feiners, and in the towns, or rather in Dublin, by a sense of the futility of all war, and in particular this war, whose aims were vague enough to the statesmen, and appeared almost illusory to the worker. Hence anyone reading the *Workers Republic* could have noticed whole passages that might have been taken direct from the German Socialist Liebknecht.

One very significant leader (Saturday, February 5, 1916) on "The Ties that Bind" is well worth quoting in parts as an example of this feeling:—

"Recently we have been pondering deeply over the ties that bind this country to England. It is not a new theme for our thoughts; for long years we have carried on propaganda in Ireland, pointing out how the strings of self-interest bound the capitalist and landlord classes to the Empire, and how it thus became a waste of time to appeal to those classes in the name of Irish patriotism.

"We have said that the working class was the only class to whom the word 'Empire,' and the things of which it was the symbol, did not appeal; that to the propertied classes 'Empire' meant high dividends and financial security, whereas to the working class that meant only the things it was in rebellion against.

"Therefore from the intelligent working class could alone come the revolutionary impulse.

"Recently we have seen the spread of those ties of self-interest binding certain classes and individuals to the Empire—we have seen it spread to a most astonishing degree until its ramifications cover the island, like the spread of a foul disease.

"It would be almost impossible to name a single class or section of the population not evilly affected by this social, political, and moral leprosy....

"For the sake of £400 a year our parliamentary representatives become Imperialists; for the sake of large travelling expenses and luxurious living they become lying recruiters....

"There is nobody in a representative position so mean that the British Government will not pay some price for his Irish soul. Newspaper men sell their Irish souls for Government advertisements paid for at a lavish rate. Professors sell their souls for salaries and expenses, clergymen sell theirs for jobs for their relatives, business men sell their souls and become recruiters lest they lose the custom of Government officials. In all the grades of Irish society the only section that has not furnished even one apostate to the cause it had worked for in times of peace is that of the much hated and traduced militant labour leaders.

"But if the militant labour leaders of Ireland have not apostatized, the same cannot be said of the working class as a whole....

"Perhaps some day the same evil passions the enemy has stirred up in so many of our Irish people will play havoc with his own hopes, and make more bitter and deadly the cup of his degradation and defeat.

"But deep in the heart of Ireland has sunk the sense of the degradation wrought upon its people—our lost brothers and sisters—so deep and humiliating that no agency less potent than the red tide of war on Irish soil will ever be able to enable the Irish race to recover its self-respect, or establish its national dignity in the face of a world horrified and scandalized by what must seem to them our national apostasy."

Now the strange thing about Ireland is her definition of "loyalty." It is not with her a species of sentimental altruism but a plain, business-like, common-sense view of her own interests, and nothing can make her change that view, for she has through centuries of disillusionment become chronically suspicious.

"I dare say I don't take the same view as you would were you in my place," wrote Mr. Birrell to the Prime Minister on January 25th. "Loyalty in Ireland is of slow growth, and the soil is uncongenial. The plant grows slowly. Landlords, grand juries, loyalist magistrates, have all gone; yet the plant grows, though slowly."

Her patriotism, on the other hand, is almost necessarily a matter of internal administration; and for this she fights with all the spirit that animated her in the past against Dane and Saxon. Hence it is quite easy for an economic grievance at once to assume the proportions of a national movement, and once it becomes resisted as such, the spirit of nationality becomes rekindled again, and it was this latter that prompted the final efforts in the evolution of the Republic.

America and Germany both contributed to intensify the spirit of nationality and gave material assistance that made the attempt at "Separatism" a practicable ideal, but it was only made possible because of the internal troubles in Ireland herself.

So long as a constitutional outlet is not afforded for such grievances, so long must unconstitutional means be appealed to; but the question which the breakdown of the old regime suggests seriously to all thinkers is whether there are not ample means within the Constitution, and I think it is the universal opinion of the more moderate that there is; and it is just these moderates whose views will be the more welcome because of the failure not merely of the Sinn Feiners to establish a Republic, but of Sir Edward Carson and John Redmond to come to an understanding that would have placed them in a position to have controlled it in time, and, which is more important still, to be able to deal with any repetition of a similar character in the future.

Probably no analysis of the remoter causes of the rebellion, however, is more accurate than the psychological origin given by George Bernard Shaw in a letter to the *Daily News* on May 10th.

"The relation of Ireland to Dublin Castle is in this respect precisely that of the Balkan States to Turkey, of Belgium or the city of Lille to the Kaiser, and of the United States to Great Britain.

"Until Dublin Castle is superseded by a National Parliament and Ireland voluntarily incorporated with the British Empire, as Canada, Australasia, and South Africa have been incorporated, an Irishman resorting to arms to achieve the independence of his country is doing only what Englishmen will do if it be their misfortune to be invaded and conquered by the

Germans in the course of the present war. Further, such an Irishman is as much in order morally in accepting assistance from the Germans in this struggle with England as England is in accepting the assistance of Russia in her struggle with Germany. The fact that he knows that his enemies will not respect his rights if they catch him, and that he must, therefore, fight with a rope round his neck, increases his risk, but adds in the same measure to his glory in the eyes of his compatriots and of the disinterested admirers of patriotism throughout the world. It is absolutely impossible to slaughter a man in this position without making him a martyr and a hero, even though the day before the rising he may have been only a minor poet. The shot Irishmen will now take their places beside Emmet and the Manchester Martyrs in Ireland, and beside the heroes or Poland and Serbia and Belgium in Europe; and nothing in heaven or on earth can prevent it."

FOOTNOTE:

[3] I give the well-known letter in its entirety, but I cannot vouch for such passages, and I know that in many cases officers were particularly distressed at having to fight Irishmen instead of Germans.

CHAPTER THE NINTH

REFLECTIONS TOWARDS RECONSTRUCTION

One of the most gratifying things about the terrible catastrophe through which we have been passing during the last few weeks is the spirit of hope which has taken the place of the spirit of despair which immediately followed the outbreak.

Ireland has ever been more of a problem suited to statesmen than to soldiers; indeed, the soldier has more often than not come in to spoil the work of the statesman, and Mr. Asquith's hurried visit to Dublin, Cork, and Belfast after John Dillon's speech was chiefly undertaken in order to prevent any repetition of the old mistake.

The need for conciliation, everybody will admit, was exceedingly urgent, for it was the admitted intention of the Sinn Feiners to put the matter to the test as to whether England held Ireland by her own free constitutional consent, or whether it was merely a permanent military occupation, like Belgium and Poland. "England is not the champion of small nations," they said. "She never was and never will be, and while she is masquerading before the world as such it is our intention, in Ireland's name, to give her the lie—yes, even though it be in our own blood."

Indeed, as I have already said, there appears to have been a belief among the Sinn Feiners that if only they could hold the capital for twelve days by force of arms they would have a sort of claim to be mentioned at the Peace Conference along with Poland and Belgium.

Now, it matters very little whether such a suggestion came from Berlin or Washington, or whether the whole thing was a fable, for the grand fact remains that England now stands before Europe with the point of Ireland's loyalty openly questioned, and she has only two courses open: she must either neglect Irish opinion and proclaim that she holds the sister isle by right of conquest—when, of course, the fate of Belgium is sealed as far as England's ethical pleading is concerned—or she may make such a final compact with Ireland that she can afterwards maintain before the whole world, without fear of contradiction, that Ireland is freely one with England without the help of a single soldier.

It's really more important than winning the war, if Englishmen could only realize it—for the psychology of Ireland is the psychology of every one of the constituent nations of our common Empire; and the late Mr. Stead used to say to me, "A blunder in Irish government is a blunder in Imperial government"; but I never realized this so much as when I learnt with what an intense interest the Indian students present in Dublin had followed the whole case.

When the Irish leader, therefore, in the acuteness of the moment expressed the hope that no party would be allowed to make capital out of the event, he expressed a hope which was re-echoed in every Irish breast; but it would have been far more effective if he had instead expressed the hope that each party should bear its proper share in the guilt of the catastrophe.

For the danger is the making of the Sinn Feiners into a national scapegoat for the faults of all.

For in a sense all were responsible. True, neither Redmondites nor Carsonites took any part in it—and it is very lucky they did not, for it would have meant civil war and fearful bloodshed from one end of the country to the other—but in neither case was it out of any love for England, for both of them fully realized that they might have been in the position of the Sinn Feiners themselves, and both were equally determined to rid Ireland of English meddlers.

It might almost be called a "tragedy of errors," for there was nothing but blundering all round. England should never have allowed Carson to arm, nor should Redmond have followed suit if he wished to play the constitutional game to the end; but once both had appealed to the principle of physical force, neither had a right to censure the methods of a third party which had arisen out of their own incapacity to keep the country in hand.

England was in principle perfectly justified in employing force against the whole three of them, and hastened to take full advantage of the situation by handing the reins of government over to the military—but that was the greatest blunder of the lot.

For there can be no doubt that to the rank and file of the Sinn Feiners, as to the rank and file of the Orangemen, physical force was not an end in itself: it was only the protest of conscientious objectors which was being lashed into activity under continual provocation—the provocation of being threatened with the loss of everything they held most dear in life, and eminently admired by Englishmen for that very fact.

Normally Sinn Feiners and Orangemen were men of peace, the one economists, the other business men, who might indeed have been easily pacified had they been openly and sympathetically treated with, instead of being galled into fury by the taunt of bluff or cowardice, and such epithets as insignificant, negligible minorities.

In an orgy of majority government both stood out for the sanctity of minorities, especially when those minorities represented inviolable principles of vital import to the majority.

It was the method of suppression that really did most of the mischief, for in addition to casualties and damages there was also considerable distress, and it at once became necessary to organize a system of food distribution and relief for the sufferers.

This was largely undertaken by the St. Vincent de Paul Society, under Sir Henry Robinson, Vice-President of the Local Government Board, and with the help of the military authorities, who lent motor-lorries and money, food was distributed to over one hundred thousand persons.

House-to-house visitations were made, and these revealed all forms of distress, from lack of food, which, of course, it had been impossible to obtain as long as the city was in a state of siege, down to absolute ruination of whole families.

In places the city looked like Antwerp during the siege, or London upon the arrival of the Belgian refugees.

No one has yet been able to estimate the full extent of the material damage sustained by the reckless bombardment of the city—for no other word can be used; and though Captain Purcell, the chief of the Dublin Fire Brigade, gave the rough figure of £2,500,000, this must be taken as a mere minimum of the extent covered by the conflagrations.

It cannot represent the loss of business, employment, goodwill, trade, and the thousand and one other losses inseparable from such a catastrophe.

Take, for example, the loss of the Royal Hibernian Academy, with thousands of pounds of pictures. No price can repay these, for they represented perhaps the culminating point, or at least the turning point, in careers which had had years of hard struggles, and which had set perhaps a lifetime's hopes upon a single canvas.

From all accounts, too, it was the merest chance that the whole northern portion of the town did not fall a victim to the devouring flames, and it is hard to understand the psychology of the military mind which could risk even the mere possibility of such an event, as it is hard to understand why the firemen were fired on by the rebels when trying to extinguish the flames.

The hardest part of it all was, moreover, that the blow fell almost entirely upon the shoulders of the innocent, viz. the merchants, tradesmen, shopkeepers, and employees, who were thus ruined at a single stroke within the space of a few hours without even a chance of a protest.

People began to ask seriously whether it had really been necessary at all, and the verdict was not always complimentary to the authorities. Mr. Healy raised the question in the House whether any such measures had ever been really necessary, considering that the rebels held such few positions, and these could have been isolated by the municipal water supply being cut off. It certainly seems plausible that some less brutal methods could have been adopted, considering the way Cork was saved from a similar catastrophe by the tact of the clergy, who would only have been too willing, and undoubtedly would have had the power, to act as mediators between the rebels and military in the name of the civil authorities and in the interests of the inhabitants principally and Ireland generally.

A very cute suggestion I heard from Mr. George Atkinson, the well-known Dublin artist, as we were preparing the cover of the present volume in his studio, struck me as particularly plausible.

"As long as the rebels were in their strongholds untouched," he said, "they were practically powerless, and could only have covered themselves with contempt and ridicule if they had been left alone.

"These men were asking for martyrdom and the glory of battle: why on earth give them their admitted object?

"They were in possession of the Post Office. Very well, but they could not have run the postal service. They were in possession of the railways. Well and good, but they would not have been able to conduct the train service. They had assumed the reins of government, but would the people of Ireland have acknowledged them? Certainly not. They had taken over the management of the capital, but were they able to police it even, or protect private property? Why, from the very first moment of their victory—if victory it could be called—the whole place had been at the mercy of the mob.

"Again, they issued receipts in the name of the Irish Republic's exchequer, but what financier would have honoured their bills? Could they have even taken the gold from the banks they could not have got credit or cash for any further transactions. They had assumed sole authority over the people of Ireland, yet they could not have commanded enough votes to secure a single constituency.

"These men, left to themselves, in fact, and treated with a sense of humour, were on the highroad to the greatest political fiasco the world had ever seen, and could only have made themselves ridiculous and contemptible in the eyes of their own countrymen and others throughout the world.

"They had appealed to Germany: very well; let them look to German help for assistance, and in the meanwhile let them know that Casement had been captured already, before the rising, and the phantom Prussian armada had been sunk to the bottom of the sea.

"What could have happened? You say 'Pillage and murder.' They were not out for that, in the first place, nor were they that type; and it may be questioned whether, had they set about it with deliberate purpose, they would have worked such havoc as the military and naval artillery wrought in that fatal week."

The theory is certainly one which would have had no precedent to recommend it, but to my mind it was just this that was its best recommendation; in fact, what was most needed was to avoid a repetition of the old fatal precedents which had turned so many futile revolts into glorious outbursts of patriotism.

Just imagine the situation. England would first of all have told them she wished for no bloodshed beyond the punishment of those who had actually shot defenceless men or whose orders had led to these murders. It would have redounded entirely to the credit of the Englishman.

England would then have asked the politicians and people alike if they in any way sympathized with such a revolt, and let the penalties be known— the immediate erasure of Home Rule from the Statute Book and the cessation of land purchase, as well as the stoppage of all commercial or financial transactions.

Finally, if these failed and the people of Ireland really wished for war in its full reality, they could have it, but they must not ever afterward appeal as constitutional partners in the Empire, but merely as a conquered race: mercy they might have, rights they would have forfeited by conquest.

Had such a course been followed, there would not only have been an opportunity upon the part of the nation at large to disown the usurpers, who would then have had not even the vestige of a grievance upon which to establish their preposterous claims to continuance in the position they had taken up.

In a word, the English would have made fools of them, or rather allowed the Irish to make fools of them. Instead of this, all the old fatal, discredited methods were employed with the same fatal results, and they became national heroes, whose suppression by force could only give them greater power.

The whole thing would have taken no longer than the campaign; no further blood would have been spilt, and time would have been allowed for the great adventure to reveal itself in the true grotesqueness of cold reality.

Possibly it was looked upon as *infra dig.* to treat with rebels, but it was so obviously a mental case that it is hard to see how anything could possibly have been *infra dig.* under such circumstances.

On Monday and Tuesday the Republic was no more representative of the people of Ireland than the tailors of Tooley Street were the people of England, but upon the old Grecian principle that the sufferings of one citizen are the sufferings of the whole State, it became national from the moment the national sentiment had been aroused by the indiscriminate shedding of blood.

It was in their defeat that the Sinn Feiners won their great victory, and they knew it. They had been scoffed at, derided, denounced by the official party almost to—in fact, actually to—a state of desperation, and an act of despair became their last resort. The Statute Book indeed proclaimed Ireland a nation once again, but the Government treated Ireland more like a province than ever, and her own representatives seemed to acquiesce; so, as Mrs. Pearse, the mother of the "President," told me afterwards, "there was nothing left for them but to accomplish the sacrifice demanded to save the soul of Ireland and proclaim her on the scaffold once again unconquered and unconquerable."

It was an act of folly, if you like, to try to set up a republic, especially during such a crisis as this war, but since the death of the leaders brought out their true character, it has ceased to be looked upon as a piece of knavery, for these men, according to all accounts of the priests, died the death of saints, not scoundrels; so that we now realize the old, old story of the tragedy of misunderstanding, as much, indeed, by their own countrymen as by the Englishman.

If it was to illustrate in one dramatic coup that misunderstanding which has been growing between all parties in Ireland, then they have not died in vain, for every party must feel to a certain extent responsible for the catastrophe. Several things, however, seem to stand out prominently amidst the chaos.

Castle government is dead as Queen Anne and Home Rule as natural and as inevitable as the morrow's sunrise; Unionism, in the English sense of Empire, survives: everyone is a Unionist now; but what still remains inexorable is the attitude of Sir Edward Carson, whose "Unionism" is merely a euphemism for "bureaucracy," and who, with the Ulster Volunteers still in arms, equally prepared to resist constitutional government, whether from Westminster or from Dublin, is the greatest Home Ruler of us all—or should we say Sinn Feiner?

Personally, I have always thought, and still think, that the Orangeman has more to gain in an Irish Parliament than anyone else as representing the layman, the business man; but I, for one, should be sorry to see Home Rule at the cost of a single Ulster Volunteer's life.

Mr. William O'Brien has for years, as a species of political outcast, been preaching the doctrine of conciliation, and has suffered in consequence, but his successful opponents have not gained the victory, for we are now rapidly drifting towards the total exclusion of several counties—the thing of all things they most wished to avoid.

All the while people are wondering whether it is the people themselves or the politicians who are responsible for the antagonism, and three of the greatest national movements since the days of tenant grievances stare us in the face as outside, if not politics, at least outside the ordinary conventional politicians—I mean Sir Horace Plunkett's Co-operative Movement, Larkin-Connolly's Labour Movement, and Sinn Fein.

Surely something is wrong if such movements cannot be assimilated by either of the great political parties, as they should have been if those parties were together completely representative of the nation.

All our greatest men were isolated—Redmond, Carson, Plunkett, O'Brien, Connolly, W. M. Murphy, the Lord-Lieutenant—all appealing to or threatening the unfortunate Premier, already sufficiently occupied with the intricacies of English politics, let alone European.

The step must come from the Englishman in his own defence: English politics must no longer be dominated by the votes or the threats of any Irishman, and some method must be found, while safeguarding the Imperial link, to force Irishmen to meet each other and settle with each other: for the only result of ruling Tipperary from Downing Street is that Westminster is ruled from Dublin or Belfast.

According to the "political correspondent" of the *Manchester Guardian*, the tendency is towards an Irish Coalition. "The question," he writes, "is not whether there will be a change. The old and anarchic system of Dublin Castle seems to be definitely doomed. The question is rather what the change will be. Speculation, which may or may not be partially informed, concentrates upon the scheme of a new Irish Advisory Council. I may offer a more detailed sketch of this scheme, of which I will only say that some responsible Irish members think it is very likely to be near the mark. An Irish Council, if created now, would probably be an advisory body, resembling the Viceroy's Council in India. The Lord-Lieutenant, who ought to be an active and energetic administrator, would no doubt preside over it. As to the membership, it would have to consist of representatives of both Irish Parties. It is thought possible that some Nationalist and Ulster Unionist members of the House of Commons would be on it, and would, of course, sit with it in Dublin. In addition there might be responsible Irish public men (like, for example, Sir Horace Plunkett), both Home Rulers and Unionists, who are not members of the House of Commons or officially attached to a party. There might also, in view of the educational problem of Ireland, be one or two representatives of the Churches. This would form what is talked of as the Irish Coalition, in which it is assumed both Mr. Redmond's Party and Sir Edward Carson's would join."

The tribute which Mr. Birrell paid to the Irish Literary Revival and its influence upon Irish life is worth quoting, for it indicates one of the sources whence much may be hoped in the work of reconstruction.

"This period," he said, referring to the period immediately preceding the rebellion, "was also marked by a genuine literary Irish revival, in prose, poetry, and the drama, which has produced remarkable books and plays, and a school of acting, all characterized by originality and independence of thought and expression, quite divorced from any political party, and all tending towards and feeding latent desires for some kind of separate Irish national existence. It was a curious situation to watch, but there was nothing in it suggestive of revolt or rebellion, except in the realm of thought. Indeed, it was quite the other way. The Abbey Theatre made merciless fun of mad political enterprise, and lashed with savage satire some historical aspects of the Irish revolutionary. I was often amazed at the literary detachment and courage of the playwright, the relentless audacity of the actors and actresses, and the patience and comprehension of the audience. This new critical tone and temper, noticeable everywhere, penetrating everything, and influencing many minds in all ranks, whilst having its disintegrating effects upon old-fashioned political beliefs and worn-out controversial phrases, was the deadly foe of that wild sentimental passion which has once more led so many brave young fellows to a certain doom, in the belief that in Ireland any revolution is better than none. A little more time, and, but for the outbreak of the war, this new critical temper would, in my belief, have finally prevailed, not indeed to destroy national sentiment (for that is immortal), but to kill by ridicule insensate revolt. But this was not to be."

With regard to "Separatism," I believe this—and I think in so saying I am echoing the sentiments of most of my fellow-countrymen, that the only way to liberate Ireland is to dominate England, not physically, for this would be as useless as it would be impossible, but mentally and morally.

If the Irishman has been persecuted and tyrannized over, it is in virtue of certain ideals and principles which are ethically and economically inferior to his, and which he has consequently to crush in the very source, as much for his own sake as for those other members of the Empire to which, if it has been a misfortune to belong in the past, it may be an advantage and an honour to belong to-morrow.

If Castle government is wrong in Dublin it is wrong elsewhere; if militarism was wrong and foolish and futile in Cromwell's day, it is wrong to-day, to-morrow, and for all time; if England really intends at the great Peace Congress to come forward as the champion of small nations, she must be able to show an Ireland prosperous, contented, and freely allied to her without the aid of a single soldier or a single threat.

Such at least is the hope of all those who believe that only when we have solved the Irish problem have we solved the problem of Empire.

Primarily, however, the task is in Ireland's own hands: for England at this moment stands not unwilling or hostile so much as perplexed and bewildered at the strange eruption that has taken place, and which must be taken rather as an indication of a chronic state than the expression of any concrete or definite complaint.

In other words, there is already a new nationalism in the making, more idealistic, more spiritual, more constructive, and more comprehensive than the old nationalism, which was to a large extent geographical, material, and traditional to an almost stifling degree: the eyes of the younger men are fixed on the future, those of the older men are fixed upon the past.

The older generation will probably die immutable in mind, like veterans, nor will they ever try to mingle, but on all sides and in every sphere the younger generation has already shaken hands.

The spirit of the two is the same, the aspirations just as intense, but their methods are different: geographical isolation is against natural evolution and "Separatism" an economic, racial, and military impossibility—this last rebellion has exploded the myth; but all this will only have the effect of changing the ever-living consciousness of nationality into different channels.

Instead of being expansive, our patriotism will tend to be more intensive: our combat with England will no longer be with arms, but with thoughts and ideas, and the nobler and the truer will win; and it is in this contest that "Sinn Fein" will come forward with new force of the "living dead." If Ireland cannot be the strongest nation, she can be the freest; if she cannot be the greatest, she can be the purest; if she cannot be the richest, she can be the happiest and the kindliest: and as Greece conquered ancient Rome, so may Ireland some day conquer England, if those ideals which were bred and nurtured within her bosom can be made to dominate the inferior Saxon till they spread throughout the world; and that is why, whatever happens, Ireland must keep her "nationality" free by whatever means lie at her hands, and that was the root cause of the revolt, if we are to believe the words of the men who suffered.

"Others have been struck before now," said Pearse in the course of an address which he delivered in October 1897 to a young men's literary society, "by the fact that hundreds of noble men and true have fought and bled for the emancipation of the Gaelic race, and yet have all failed. Surely, if ever cause was worthy of success, it was the cause for which Laurence prayed, for which Hugh of Dungannon planned, for which Hugh Roe and Owen Roe fought, for which Wolfe Tone and Lord Edward and Robert Emmet gave their lives, for which Grattan pleaded, for which Moore and Davis sang, for which O'Connell wore himself out with toil. Yet these men prayed and planned, and fought and bled, and pleaded and wrote and toiled in vain. May it not be that there is some reason for this? May it not be that the ends they struggled for were ends never intended for the Gael?... The Gael is not like other men; the spade and the loom and the sword are not for him. But a destiny more glorious than that of Rome, more glorious than that of Britain, awaits him: to become the saviour of idealism in modern intellectual and social life, the regenerator and rejuvenator of the literature of the world, the instructor of the nations, the preacher of the gospel of nature-worship, hero-worship, God-worship—such is the destiny of the Gael."

Milton Keynes UK
Ingram Content Group UK Ltd.
UKHW042226180324
439698UK00005B/499

9 789357 958943